SHRIMP

Edible

Series Editor: Andrew F. Smith

EDIBLE is a revolutionary series of books dedicated to food and drink that explores the rich history of cuisine. Each book reveals the global history and culture of one type of food or beverage.

Already published

Apple Erika Janik · *Banana* Lorna Piatti-Farnell
Barbecue Jonathan Deutsch and Megan J. Elias
Beef Lorna Piatti-Farnell · *Beer* Gavin D. Smith
Brandy Becky Sue Epstein · *Bread* William Rubel
Cake Nicola Humble · *Caviar* Nichola Fletcher
Champagne Becky Sue Epstein · *Cheese* Andrew Dalby
Chillies Heather Arndt Anderson · *Chocolate* Sarah Moss
and Alexander Badenoch · *Cocktails* Joseph M. Carlin
Corn Michael Owen Jones · *Curry* Colleen Taylor Sen
Dates Nawal Nasrallah · *Doughnut* Heather Delancey Hunwick
Dumplings Barbara Gallani · *Edible Flowers* Constance L. Kirker
and Mary Newman · *Eggs* Diane Toops · *Fats* Michelle Phillipov
Figs David C. Sutton · *Game* Paula Young Lee · *Gin* Lesley Jacobs
Solmonson · *Hamburger* Andrew F. Smith · *Herbs* Gary Allen
Herring Kathy Hunt · *Honey* Lucy M. Long · *Hot Dog* Bruce Kraig
Ice Cream Laura B. Weiss · *Lamb* Brian Yarvin · *Lemon* Toby Sonneman
Lobster Elisabeth Townsend · *Melon* Sylvia Lovegren · *Milk* Hannah Velten
Moonshine Kevin R. Kosar · *Mushroom* Cynthia D. Bertelsen
Nuts Ken Albala · *Offal* Nina Edwards · *Olive* Fabrizia Lanza
Onions and Garlic Martha Jay · *Oranges* Clarissa Hyman
Oyster Carolyn Tillie · *Pancake* Ken Albala · *Pasta and Noodles*
Kantha Shelke · *Pie* Janet Clarkson · *Pineapple* Kaori O'Connor
Pizza Carol Helstosky · *Pomegranate* Damien Stone · *Pork* Katharine
M. Rogers · *Potato* Andrew F. Smith · *Pudding* Jeri Quinzio
Rice Renee Marton · *Rum* Richard Foss · *Salad* Judith Weinraub
Salmon Nicolaas Mink · *Sandwich* Bee Wilson · *Sauces* Maryann Tebben
Sausage Gary Allen · *Seaweed* Kaori O'Connor · *Shrimp* Yvette Florio Lane
Soup Janet Clarkson · *Spices* Fred Czarra · *Sugar* Andrew F. Smith
Tea Helen Saberi · *Tequila* Ian Williams · *Truffle* Zachary Nowak
Vodka Patricia Herlihy · *Water* Ian Miller
Whiskey Kevin R. Kosar · *Wine* Marc Millon

Shrimp

A Global History

Yvette Florio Lane

REAKTION BOOKS

For Wendi Harris Kaufman (1964–2014), who loved stories

Published by Reaktion Books Ltd
Unit 32, Waterside
44–48 Wharf Road
London N1 7UX, UK
www.reaktionbooks.co.uk

First published 2017
Copyright © Yvette Florio Lane 2017

Printed and bound in China by 1010 Printing International Ltd

A catalogue record for this book is available from the British Library

ISBN 978 1 78023 849 4

Contents

Introduction: Endless Shrimp?

Shrimp – or, if you prefer, prawns – are the world's most popular shellfish, and one of the ocean's most sought-after foods. Whether they are the featured protein in the main meal or the crucial addictive element in popular snack foods, shrimp are the world's most-consumed crustacean. It is no surprise that they are so universally desired – they are tasty, nutritious and quickly prepared. With their crisp yet yielding texture, and their mild and slightly salty, slightly sweet flesh, shrimp also lend themselves to any number of culinary styles and preparations, and are pleasing to a broad range of palates.

An incredibly adaptive species, shrimp thrive in salt water and in fresh, in warm water as well as cold – from the frigid North Sea to the swampy Louisiana Bayou to the mangrove forests of Asia and Latin America. Subsequently, they have landed in fishing nets and cooking pots around the globe, and untold numbers are served each day at the world's tables. And yet, for all their geographic abundance, actually procuring enough shrimp for an adequate meal takes some doing. Owing to their relative scarcity, their need for constant and reliable refrigeration (or immediate preservation through other means) and the effort required to transport them over long distances, shrimp also have been used as a barometer of class, wealth and status through the ages. In the value-priced, all-you-can-eat, farm-raised global shrimp market of today, the problem is not that there is too much, but that there is not enough.

Over the centuries, shrimp have played a part over the centuries as culinary ambassadors, carrying novel cooking methods and flavours on their tiny backs. Otherwise adversarial actors have sometimes demonstrated good will, eased a fractious path and showed generosity of spirit, hospitality and common (if grudging) respect through the sharing of this commodity.

The small but mighty shrimp has been luring men and women not only in gastronomic matters, but in music, poetry and art. They have been praised as aphrodisiacs, cherished as both delicacy and luxury, and invoked as an insult. These primordial-looking creatures, which typically spend their short lives out of sight down on the sea floor, have inspired many an outsized passion.

The history of shrimp is more than just a story about a popular food. It is also a story about exclusion and power, about wealth and poverty, and about the change from a basically rural world to one transformed by modernization in the form of the petroleum engine and capitalism. Commercial shrimp fishing and farming have been plagued from the beginning by labour abuses, ecological destruction and racism. The story of shrimp is also one of shifting global power. As the twentieth century became the 'American Century' through industrial and economic might, the story of this shellfish became an increasingly American one. American inventors and innovators took control of the shrimp industry and held on to it. From shipbuilding to frozen food technology to tourism, America led the way. For some, shrimp truly were 'pink gold'. But the tide is again shifting, and the story is now turning towards Asia, as farm-raised shrimp become a multi-billion-dollar business there.

Shrimp have only become ubiquitous – and cheap – in the last thirty or so years. The Chinese have been farming shrimp since the fifteenth century, but it has taken many centuries more to create the type of large-scale aquaculture system now found in parts of Southeast Asia, India and Latin America. While today's shrimp-farming industry produces shrimp in the billions, it takes a huge toll on the surroundings – both human and environmental. It also brings with it potential health hazards and ethical dilemmas for those who consume its products. Wild-caught shrimp, much of it procured through trawling, is not much better, as it leaves another type of ecological nightmare in its wake, tearing up the ocean floor and destroying hundreds of species of sea life, or 'bycatch', that is wasted in the process. The tireless quest for our favourite shellfish comes at a very high price.

In the not-too-distant past, a diner in a fine restaurant might have been served a smallish portion of impeccably fresh shrimp, hand-peeled and deveined, and procured at a relatively high cost from a reliable fishmonger. What often now takes its place is farm-raised, imported, frozen-and-thawed and low-priced. In the not-too-distant future, it may well be that responsibly or organically farmed varieties – higher in price and lower in environmental costs – will be the new 'status' shrimp.

Shrimp are big business – they are one of the few foodstuffs that are a tradable commodity in the world's markets. While they are enjoyed almost everywhere, in nearly every cuisine, the United States, the European Union and Japan now claim the lion's share of the fresh product. Ever since humans first pulled the pale and squirming creatures out of the rivers, lakes and oceans and put them to the fire they have wanted more. The challenge of the twenty-first century will be to keep a healthy and sustainable supply for future generations if they are to remain a part of the rich culinary heritage of the world's cultures.

I

What's in a Name? The Biology and Biography of the Shrimp

I chanced at breakfast the other day to wish I knew
something of the biography of a shrimp.
John Ruskin

Almost the first thing some people wonder when eyeing the bite-sized shellfish that seems to appear on at least one canapé platter at every social function, or pop up in a carton of noodles at many casual luncheons, is whether they are about to devour a shrimp or a prawn. To most consumers, who enjoy up to 85 per cent of their annual portion of the tasty, ten-legged crustacean in restaurants, shrimp and prawns look more or less alike. They may differ somewhat in size from dish to dish, but they share the characteristic crescent shape, the somewhat striated and opaque white meat, and the mottled and pinkish outer surface – all packed into a pliable shell. In most cases, they already have been peeled, cleaned and deveined, and if any bit of shell remains, it is a piece of the tail, helpful for keeping fingers free of any accompanying sauce.

The succulent bite dangling from a pair of chopsticks or enrobed in coconut is made up of the fellow's six muscular abdominal segments. It is what is left when everything else – the head, the legs, the reproductive and respiratory organs and exoskeleton – is stripped away. Once cooked, the flesh of all culinary shrimp turns pearly white with undertones of blue or grey, and they acquire the peachy pink outer colouration for which they are known. The exoskeleton is the shell that houses the soft body. These can range in hue from creamy yellows to greys and browns and blues, yet they all contain the pigment astaxanthin, which, when heated, turns the translucent shell to pink or red, and stains the outer flesh with its characteristic stripes. Appearance can be influenced by other factors, including the age of the shrimp, its diet, the season of harvest and the amount of time it has spent out of the water. Different types of shrimp will offer particular culinary attributes, such as the degree of crunchiness or the predominance of the taste of iodine. Many people prefer the flavour of wild-caught varieties, but others maintain that farmed shrimp can be equally delicious. Refrigeration concentrates and intensifies 'shrimpiness'.

Yes, that is all well and good, the inquisitor persists; but is it a shrimp or a prawn? Well, that depends. Some maintain that the preferred term in the UK is 'prawn', while in the U.S. it is 'shrimp', and others argue that 'prawn' indicates a larger or more robust entity. No doubt there is some truth in this, but it is far from a hard and fast rule, and in short order contradictory examples can be found to disprove the previous claim.[1]

The more interesting question might be: what is a shrimp (or a prawn) at all? The small sea animal is, technically, a member of the subphylum Crustacea. Along with lobsters and crabs, their ten-legged relatives, shrimp and prawns belong in the order Decapoda, meaning that they have five pairs of legs on the upper part of the body (which is called the carapace)

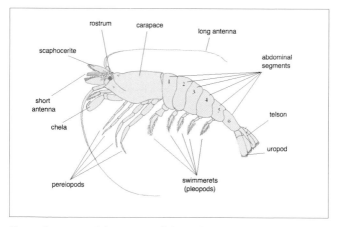

External anatomy of the common shrimp, *Crangon crangon.*

and another five pairs of legs, known as swimmerets (owing to their obvious function), on the abdomen.[2]

According to marine biologists, there are more than 2,000 types of shrimp, but only thirty or so of those are commercially available today. All belong to one of two families, both subgroups of the decapods: the larger Penaeidae and the generally smaller Caridea. While both families contain some of the most important varieties in terms of global production and consumption today, the warm-water Penaeidae are commercially dominant. The Caridea are often known as cold water shrimp and can be very small indeed. They include non-edible varieties such as brine shrimp and fairy shrimp, but also the popular wild-caught grey shrimp (*Crangon crangon*) found throughout much of Europe.

As to the original question regarding the difference between the shrimp and the prawn, even carcinologists, the slightly sinisterly named zoologists who study crustaceans (the sea creature the crab and cancer the disease share the same root word), quibble over just where to draw the line

Shrimp in its natural state.

distinguishing one type of shelled, water-dwelling swimming animal from the next. The consensus is that the terms can be used interchangeably to mean any species identified by the United Nations Food and Agriculture Organization (FAO) as edible decapods of the Natantia, that is, a swimming (as opposed to walking) suborder. As long as we are talking about the same general sort of animal, and *not* a spiny lobster, crayfish, langoustine or some other interloper, my 'shrimp' is your 'prawn', and vice versa. Regional variations and historical usage have more to do with it than any scientific criteria. Most agree that if it looks like a shrimp, and moves like a shrimp, it is a shrimp. Or a prawn. In any case, a shrimp should definitely not look like a lobster or a crab. Thus the words 'shrimp' and 'prawn' have no biological specificity, but are merely a matter of geography and habit.

This linguistic sauce thickens, however, when non-Anglophone words are brought to bear. According to the list of aquatic species provided by the FAO, the popular *Penaeus*

FISH.

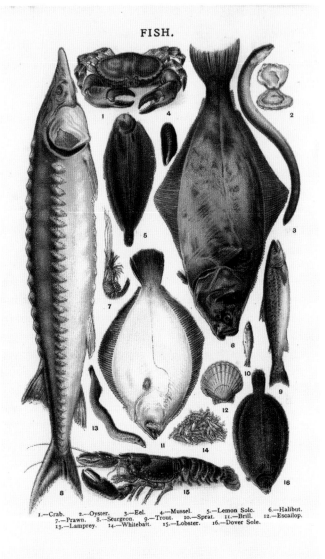

1.—Crab. 2.—Oyster. 3.—Eel. 4.—Mussel. 5.—Lemon Sole. 6.—Halibut.
7.—Prawn. 8.—Sturgeon. 9.—Trout. 10.—Sprat. 11.—Brill. 12.—Escailop.
13.—Lamprey. 14.—Whitebait. 15.—Lobster. 16.—Dover Sole.

Nineteenth-century print of sea creatures.

vannamei, known in English as the whiteleg shrimp, is rendered in French as *crevettes à pattes blanches*, and in Spanish as *camarón patiblanco*. Yet the similarly much-desired giant tiger prawn is known to the international authorities by its formal Latin name, *Penaeus monodon*, while to the French chef it is *crevette géante tigrée*, but simply *langostino jumbo* to the Spanish speaker. The attentive reader surely will have noticed that here the Spaniard uses the noun *langostino* rather than *camarón* (shrimp), even though the more common word for prawn is *gamba*. Thus someone unfamiliar with the nuances of a particular language's seafood varieties would be hard pressed to know from the name alone whether to expect a shrimp, a prawn or a langoustine to arrive on one's plate.

In the UK, the Norway lobster (or langoustine) is also known as scampi or, more confusingly, a Dublin Bay prawn. In the U.S., a request for an order of 'shrimp scampi' brings forth a dish composed of whole shrimp sautéed and served in a sauce of garlic, butter, olive oil, white wine and sometimes cheese. Typically, this salty and oily love match is served over pasta or rice. It is so enshrined in the culture as a suitable meal for special events and first dates that it is on the menu of any Italian-American restaurant worth its salt, is among the perennial best-sellers at national seafood and Italian-style chain restaurants, and is even recognized in an ersatz holiday, National Shrimp Scampi Day, which is (ostensibly) observed on 29 April each year. This dish does not exist in Italy, where shrimp are known as *gamberi*, and *scampi* are langoustines.

In Venice, where the *scampi* (plural of *scampo*) favour the local Adriatic waters, they are often prepared in a simple garlic and oil sauté and served with risotto. When Italian immigrants to America found shrimp more readily available, and langoustines much less so, they did what émigrés often do when seeking to reproduce the tastes of the old country.

They improvised. Instead of langoustines, they served shrimp, prepared in the style of (*alla*) scampi, sautéed with olive oil and garlic. And they adapted and truncated its name, American-style, into 'shrimp scampi'. At its best, it is a dish of such simplicity and near universal approval that it should be in the repertoire of every home cook. It is less a recipe than a method, and when paired with a bracing green vegetable, it serves as a primer for putting a proper meal together in about twenty minutes.

So while most agree that differences do exist between the shrimp and the prawn, they are of such little culinary consequence as to make drawing a distinction in terms a pointless exercise in hair-splitting. Now, this is not to say that all decapods, be they prawns or shrimp, will be exactly the same in taste, texture or appearance. It only means that whatever term one chooses to use is of little consequence and should be the cause of no stigma, shame or embarrassment for possibly

Shrimp 'scampi' style with pasta.

having erred. Freshness, quality, size, availability and personal preference should be the guide.

If this seems a rather imprecise way to embark on a serious treatment of the subject at hand, it is worth considering the subject of crustacean nomenclature, and seafood labelling in general, before going any further. It all appears hopeless, and it has only been made more so by a recent change in scientific classification. Naming challenges aside, what is much more worrying is that the obfuscation that confounds the consumer is often in the best interest of whoever stands to make a profit. Absent a universally recognized vocabulary with standardized measurements and definitions and enforceable regulations, labels such as 'organic', 'wild-caught' and 'natural' are as useless as descriptions as 'hand-crafted' and 'farm fresh'.

Although they can be pricier per pound than other protein sources, shrimp are also supremely economical. Almost every bit can be used to impart flavour. Even the shells themselves can be consumed, although unless they are very thin, chewing through them can be unpleasant. The question of what to do with the shells has preoccupied cooks for centuries. If the shrimp are not peeled before cooking, in order to maintain optimal flavour or to save time, this then poses an etiquette challenge. One is left with the dilemma of removing the shell at table or consuming it.

In 1845 Eliza Acton, the fifth child of a Sussex brewer, wrote the first cookbook that was really meant for the housewife and not the professional cook. Acton was a romantic poet of moderate success and an unlikely cookbook author. On the advice of her publisher, she wrote *Modern Cookery for Private Families*, which opened the way for the entire genre of prescriptive literature that followed, from *Mrs Beeton* to *Good Housekeeping* to *Martha Stewart Living*. Acton's great innovation was to include, in a separate section, precise quantities and cooking times for her recipes. It remained in print until 1914, and was one of the most influential cookbooks ever published. On the subject of shrimp shells she observed:

To Shell Shrimps and Prawns Quickly and Easily

This, though a most simple process, would appear, from the manner in which it is performed by many people, to be a very difficult one; indeed, it is not unusual for persons of the lower classes, who, from lack of a little skill, find it slow and irksome, to have resource to the dangerous plan of eating the fish entire. It need scarcely be remarked that very serious consequences may accrue from the shells being swallowed with them, particularly when they are taken in large quantities.

Indeed, it is easy to remove the shell, and usually worth the small amount of extra time, although it is not desirable in all recipes. Some dishes actually call for the shrimp to be cooked in and eaten with the seasoned shell. The idea is that the shell adds an arresting textural dimension and the shell itself is highly flavoured (Chinese pepper shrimp with shells on is one well-known dish). It is not for everyone.

In the countries of the West, shrimp are often sold raw with the shell still on and head already removed and discarded – what is known as 'green' shrimp. In much of Asia, but also in Latin America and in parts of Europe, where freshness and flavour are the primary concerns, shrimp are usually purchased with shell and heads intact. The Spanish dish *gambas al ajillo* famously leaves the heads on to impart the bitter juice, said to give the requisite savour. Those flavourful bits can be removed before serving the prepared dish, although often are

'Green' shrimp: heads off, raw, shells on.

not. The preference for headless shrimp in many Western cultures emerged near the middle of the twentieth century when machine technology first made the shelling and heading process faster and cheaper, but now it is firmly established, and the first sighting of the thing in the rough can be rather discomfiting for the uninitiated. If shrimp with heads on are available, by all means, purchase them. Most likely they have not been frozen. The heads are easy to remove and will add immeasurably to any dish that is prepared with them.

Most cooks prefer to purchase shrimp with the shell still on. In the first place, the shell preserves the freshness and flavour of the meat and prevents damage. In the second, smart and thrifty cooks know that shrimp shells (heads included) make the best stock for cream or tomato sauces or soups, stews, risottos and marinades. The shells are filled with sugars, which, when heated with a cooking liquid, release easily. Shrimp butter is another way to make a silk purse out of something that otherwise might have gone to waste. (Never, but never, put them into a waste disposal unit. Discard unwanted shells in a rubbish bin with other organic waste according to local recycling law.) It is a straightforward process of smashing the peelings from the cooked shrimp (which retain much of their flavour), together with a bit of tomato paste, into butter until they are nearly completely incorporated, and then pushing the rose-coloured mass through a sieve to remove any small shards that escaped the onslaught. It takes only a bit of elbow grease to finish – 'just pound,' commanded Julia Child in *Mastering the Art of French Cooking* (1961). She conceded that a blender and melted butter would work well, too.

The shells also make a nitrogen-rich fertilizer. For the eminently practical home economist, the shells can be added to compost with just a few steps of labour to prepare them. The main drawback in composting shells is that they produce a strong fishy odour, but this can be reduced by either boiling them before composting, or by covering the shells with a thin

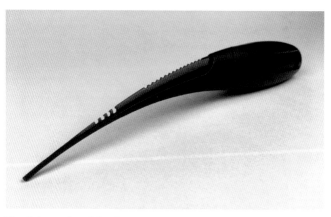

Deveining tool used for cleaning shrimp.

layer of leaves or grass clippings after they have been added to the compost bin or pile. In fact, the shells make such a good fertilizing agent that Chinese migrants to California in the nineteenth century built a thriving export business shipping them back to China specifically for that use.

The amount of shells dumped each year is staggering. Taken together, the shell and the head make up between 40 and 60 per cent of the shrimp's total body weight. It is true that they are biodegradable, but they still pose a significant nuisance, if not an outright health threat, to communities that are inundated with millions of pounds of them. The shells smell and attract insects, and they clog water drainage systems. Recovering and reusing them could add to the income of shrimp farmers, reduce waste and free up resources for other uses.

Because they are made primarily of chitin (a type of naturally occurring polymer), when chitin-eating bacteria digest them they release compounds into the soil which may confer beneficial properties – another reason why they make excellent fertilizer. Chitin is not all that can be recovered from the discarded shells. Proteins, too, are abundant. These can be made into animal feed, with possibilities extending even to human food uses envisaged down the road. Chitin itself is a bit of a wonder product, with applications in medicine, engineering and industry just beginning to be explored.[3]

Researchers at Harvard's Wyss Institute have even used the shells to create a new polymer they are hoping will replace plastic bags and other disposable items. They have named it 'shrilk' because it is made by combining the shrimp protein with another protein found in silk. With a bit of engineering and ingenuity, shrimp shells may soon have their own metamorphosis and a second life.

2

How We Do Love Thee

For the most part, food historians assume that people around the world have welcomed shrimp into their everyday diet as both a seasonal and secondary source of protein and, significantly, as a special and rare food used to celebrate major life events. There were some notable exceptions to this. Icelanders and Russians, for example, did not consider shrimp desirable until after the Second World War, even though peoples all around them did. Others forbade it on religious grounds. As a natural and wild product, its availability and abundance waxes and wanes. The only practical way to catch shrimp was with nets or baskets, cast or trawled by hand along the shore when the shrimp moved locations during their spawning and maturation processes. This required luck and timing. Baskets, nets and other accoutrements were made by hand following age-old practices. This material culture indicates that people had the technology and the desire to invest time and resources into harvesting shrimp, and it appears that this happened almost everywhere in the world and very far back into human history.

In many ways, however, the history of shrimp is also a divided one. Perhaps it is best to think of shrimp as having two separate historical epochs, one before it became a commercially produced and distributed commodity, and one after. Until around the turn of the twentieth century, shrimp was largely a local and occasional food for people who lived near the fresh and saline waterways that provided it naturally. With their tough outer shells, multiple squirmy legs and weird eyes, it is reasonable to wonder who first dared to take a bite of this particular blue-blooded water creature. We will never know. Since the delicate exoskeletons decompose quickly, and physiological traces essentially vanish, it is impossible to determine with certainty where, when and in what quantity early people consumed them. Unlike the shells of molluscs, which withstand the elements and are found in giant waste mounds archaeologists call 'middens', the softer outer cuticle of shrimp does not stand up to the passage of time. It was not until archaeologists finally uncovered evidence such as fossil-ized mouth parts of shrimp, as well as material culture includ-ing clay drying bowls, that they could confidently conclude that freshwater varieties had been a significant source of protein for the Aztecs in Mexico before large meat-giving species of mammals were transported to Meso-America by the European invaders.

The oldest written records listing penaeid varieties have been found in China, going back to sometime between the eighth and second centuries BCE. Shrimp dishes have featured prominently in many Asian cuisines, and are still considered essential to New Year's celebrations, in part because of the shrimp's auspicious red colour and its curved back, which is said to resemble the hunched posture acquired in old age – a sign of longevity.

Turning towards the West, the ancient Greeks were sur-rounded by water; no point lay more than 136 km (85 mi.) from the sea, and shrimp were part of a cuisine abundant with seafood. Along with the famous triad of wheat, olive oil

Japanese New Year's greeting postcard, early 20th century.

and wine on which so much of Mediterranean cuisine relies, Greeks made ample use of the fermented fish sauce known as *garum*. They combined *garum* with honey to make a sweet and salty glaze for grilled shrimp, not unlike barbecue sauces popular today. More elegant dishes were prepared with shrimp wrapped and cooked in fig or grape leaves. Later, the classical world brought forth shrimp-lover par excellence Marcus Gavius Apicius. Apicius lived in Rome during the first century CE, and has been described as history's first gourmet or 'foodie', but he has also been labelled, probably more accurately, a glutton. He is chiefly remembered today because his collected writings, *De re coquinaria* (On the Subject of Cooking), compiled four to five centuries after his death, are said to be the font from which all subsequent Western cookery books flow – but their authorship and authenticity are in question.

Apicius was known for his outsized displays, on which he spent lavish amounts of money in search of the novel and grandiose. He enjoyed entertaining his frequent dinner guests with extravagant meals he himself had prepared, featuring such oddments as flamingo tongues. Much of his notoriety stems from an epic – and perhaps apocryphal – tantrum he threw in a thwarted food quest, and as a result his name will be linked with shrimp for all posterity. Following a tip that Libya was the source of the largest *squilla* (the Roman word for shrimp) in the known world, he hired a ship and a crew and set off from his home on the Italian peninsula hoping to stock up. Just before landfall on the continent, he somehow received word that the North African article was no more impressive than the Italian variety. Without seeking any proof, he ordered the ship to turn around and sailed back across the Mediterranean Sea, empty-handed. It was indeed a costly and foolish fishing expedition. This story does not tell us much about how ancient Romans ate their shrimp, except that they seemed to like them enormous – as they did a great many other things. And, despite all appearances to the contrary, they also loved a good moralizing tale. Apicius, with his impetuous voyage for the colossal Libyan shrimp, imparts a favourite Roman-style warning against luxury: do not be consumed by one's own appetites.

Poor Apicius died as he lived. When his funds eventually ran dry, forcing an end to his unsustainable style of living, he embarked on one last alimentary misadventure, and swallowed a lethal dose of poison. Aside from serving as an object lesson, Apicius' legacy includes some recipes that have been restored and made available to modern cooks, should they wish to approximate an ancient gustatory experience. As did most of his contemporaries, Apicius made liberal use of *garum*. Approximately 75 per cent of the recipes in the *coquinaria* use it. The Romans have been branded with an unfair reputation for having had appalling taste in food, largely due to their preference for what is often misread as 'rotten fish'.

Garum was probably very similar to the fish sauces used today in many Southeast Asian cuisines and found in every supermarket. Once thought to be reserved for the wealthy, it is now believed that *garum* was as widely used as tomato ketchup is today. Several citizens of Pompeii grew rich turning out buckets of the stuff and shipping it throughout Rome. When modern tourists visit Pompeii, much of what they see are the material remains of a people who lived to a higher standard than many of their neighbours, and some of that is owed to the thriving local fish sauce business that employed thousands of workers.[1]

Apicius' seafood recipes consist mainly of seafood minces combined with *garum* and black pepper and some savoury herbs. These are then shaped into patties or croquettes and fried in pork fat. It is likely that Apicius' shrimp patty, served perhaps with rice and a sweet-and-sour dipping sauce, would not seem at all unusual today.

Not all ancient peoples revered this gift of the sea as much as the Graeco-Romans. The Jewish proscription against eating shrimp has its foundation in Mosaic Law, and comes

Roman cameo gem, 1st century AD.

from Leviticus 11:9–12, which forbids the consumption of all shellfish and fish that do not have fins and scales. This, of course, rules out all molluscs, including oysters, clams, lobster and shrimp, as well as such fish as catfish and carp. Shrimp, like other decapods, are omnivores and many are 'filter feeders', meaning that they strain the solid particles from the water – whatever those particles may be. In addition, they eat parasites and the necrotic tissue of other fish. Understandably, many people view this as undesirable. For this reason they have earned the reputation of being unclean, or *treif*. It is also why some people refuse to eat shrimp today, outside of religious doctrine, owing to concerns about water contamination and other environmental hazards.

That notwithstanding, there are many (but certainly not all) Muslims who deem shrimp and prawns (those which are shrimp by another name) halal, that is, permissible to eat, and do so in accord with the Quran, Islam's book of law. Sources that advise the faithful on which foods are allowed and which are proscribed often note that it is only shrimp which are halal; prawns, that is, the kind that are *not* shrimp, are haram and forbidden. This discrepancy is most likely a result of the linguistic inconsistency in naming various sea creatures. In this case, what is meant by 'prawn' is surely the langoustine, which, with its two front claws and elongated body, looks a great deal like the haram lobster. This is where it pays to know a bit more about the thing on offer than just the fishmongers' nickname for it. But – even when the item in question is doubtlessly a proper shrimp – interpretations of scripture differ as to whether it is indeed allowed. As in all such matters of individual conscience, where the stakes are of consequence, wisdom suggests seeking a higher authority.

So while the shrimp's dietary habits cause some to shun it, some see virtue where others do not, as in the case of a nineteenth-century Christian minister and naturalist who, contemplating the very purpose of the shrimp, reminded readers that its part in the 'cosmic economy' was more than simply providing something 'to be eaten with tea and bread and butter'. He pointed out to readers that 'The sea is filled with living beings, myriads of which die daily,' and 'Unless some means existed by which their dead bodies could be removed, the water would be polluted and unable to sustain life.' This would indeed be problematic. He maintained that rather than condemn the shrimp as unclean, all should be grateful for them. While the individual shrimp may appear insignificant, when in force, it is part of 'the great army of scavengers which has been appointed for the purification of the sea', and thus, 'of the highest importance, and could not be spared without disturbing the whole economy of Nature'.[2] Of course, among that army were untold billions who had given their lives for the less noble, but beloved, tea time treat of shrimp paste on toast, although it is not clear from the treatise if one were to be forgiven for thinking that shrimp nevertheless made a fine breakfast. Yet this was an early awareness of the vital role shrimp have in maintaining the ecological balance of the sea.

In any event, it does not appear that problems of conscience weighed too heavily on very many in Western Europe, at least where the consumption of *Crangon crangon* was concerned (although associations with waterborne cholera and ptomaine poisoning would put many off shrimp well into the twentieth century). These small grey shrimp were found in abundance along the coastal regions in Europe and in some rivers and estuaries as well, and were enjoyed in huge numbers by rich and poor alike.

When the topic turns to abundance, naturally the rotund English king Henry VIII comes to mind. Before the break with

Augustus Wall Callcott (1779–1844), scene of shrimper on the coast.

Rome, and while still cutting a sharp athletic figure, he sat down to a semi-private 'fish day' (opposed to a 'flesh day', that is, meat) meal 'in the chamber' with but himself, 'the queen and courtiers', for which the second course of the lengthy 'suggested bill of fare' included 'shrimps' among the other fish and seafoods.[3] As a rule, affairs of state felled nearly every creature of field and stream and placed it upon the menu. At the coronation feast of George I, there appeared 'no less than 1,445 dishes of various viands', and cold shrimps numbered among the 145 dishes presented at His Majesty's table.

In 1660 Robert May, author of the first English book of recipes compiled by a professional cook, proffered an 'Extravagant Bride's Pye' consisting of multiple pastry cases of diminishing circumference, to be assembled in a great tower of pie. Chef May provided instructions for one sweetened case to be filled with 'prawns and cockles', along with 'a few pickled mushrooms (if you have them)'. After this layer was baked, it was to be doused with a kind of sauce composed of butter, vinegar and the costly imported ingredients orange juice and nutmeg. It was then to be placed in the stack of sturdy pies nearer the top, furthest from the meat fillings that were at the base. The entire thing was meant to resemble a rose when all was assembled.

Another of the pastry cases in the pie tower was to contain a live snake or 'a few birds'. The chef advised prospective bakers that indeed it 'will seem strange to the beholders, which cut up the pie at the Table' when the creatures are released. But, he cautioned, 'This is only for a Wedding to pass away the time.' Whatever else was occurring at that time which so caused the guests to lose their interest in the meal at hand and give rise to the need for this live wildlife show he did not divulge.[4] Already by the mid-seventeenth century, however, shrimp was a necessary food for impressing restive wedding guests.

Almost two centuries later, in 1839, a simpler and far more practicable bake was suggested by the editors of the *Magazine of Domestic Economy*. Even these authors could seem overambitious at times, as when they wrote that a 'delicious shrimp pie' was within reach of even a poor man whose wife, with just a few pennies, could buy a fresh quart of shrimp from a street peddler, and who would then be able to put together a meal sufficient for three in rapid fashion. All she had to do, once she had bargained with the shrimp man, was simply clean the shrimp, whip up a short pastry dough and gravy, line a pie pan with the pastry, pile in the shrimp, add some ketchup and butter, lay on the top crust, walk it to the neighbourhood bakehouse, where another payment would be needed to finish the job, and then, finally, pick it up again when it was fully baked. And, oh, yes, the pie should be eaten hot.[5] The editors presented this recipe as an economical and easy dish, not a special or celebratory one. Of course we cannot know how many women made this pie or only dreamed of it. It is always a challenge to locate voices that reflect what ordinary people actually ate. A handwritten cookbook, compiled sometime in the years between 1694 and 1831, in which a Mrs Johnson (or her mother) wrote down two of her shrimp recipes, one for potted shrimps and one for pickled shrimp, survives and may offer some insight. Although we do not know if Mrs Johnson actually prepared or even if she enjoyed these dishes, she thought them worthy of preserving.[6] They are simple fare, but even so, with an education and access to writing materials, domestic help and the leisure time to pen her daily remembrances, Mrs Johnson's economic circumstances put her beyond the category of the woman who went to a public bakehouse for lack of her own cooking stove.

People living anywhere near the coast, or even brackish water, like that in parts of the River Thames, enjoyed a local species of grey shrimp, that 'most popular dainty', which, according to an 1890 article in the London newspaper *The Graphic*, were eaten in 'myriads'. During the Victorian era,

French women seining for shrimp with large nets, early 20th-century postcard.

Belgian horseback shrimp fisherman, 20th-century postcard.

riverboat sailing trips became a popular holiday pastime and resort towns such as Gravesend catered to day-trippers who came in search of shrimp – either to purchase it for the return trip home, or to treat themselves to a famed 'shrimp tea', which was really the whole point of going on the excursion.[7]

Across the channel, the Belgian beach resort of Oost-duinkerke sits by the military and civilian cemeteries where thousands of fallen soldiers and fishermen lay in repose. In days past, shrimpers on horseback in this area of Belgium, *pêcheurs de crevettes aux chevaux*, dragged their nets behind them, trawling the ocean bottom, only as far out into the water as the horses would venture. They then packed the day's catch into purpose-made baskets attached to the animals' flanks. This was both a picturesque and an efficient method to be sure, so effective that it has led to overfishing and all but the destruction of a tradition that is said to have existed there since 800 CE. It is still carried out today by the ten or so *pêcheurs* who remain, but it is mainly for the tourist trade, and the United Nations Educational, Scientific and Cultural

Fried shrimp vendor, Charleston, South Carolina, early 20th-century postcard.

Organization (UNESCO) recognizes it as one of just a few types of artisanal fishing still practised today.

In Calais, women in long bathing costumes wielded what look like oversized butterfly nets attached to the end of long wooden poles. These heavy seining nets were used to capture shrimp near the surface. They would be cast into the surf to pull the shrimp up and out. It took a deft swing of powerful arms to land the net neatly on the water's surface without it folding or twisting in on itself. Similar nets were carried across the ocean to shrimping communities in the southern United States, brought there by migrants from Brittany. The earliest examples of hand-knitted nets like these have been found in Louisiana and are dated from 1735, when it was still a French colony. Their descendants would be among the men and women who developed that area into the most important shrimp-producing part of the world by the end of the next century.

Access to shrimp was not solely determined by geography, however. Proximity to the water did not ensure a bounty for all. The ability to take food from the land is never a simple and uncontested right. Along with the privilege of using the waterways, shrimping required equipment, skills and knowledge. Shrimp species vary in behaviour and habits. Knowing the best times to catch them and where there was likely to be a cache comes with experience and familiarity with the terrain.

Technology offered opportunities but limitations as well. Catching only with seine nets meant a smaller harvest, but owning or maintaining a boat required an outlay of cash. Shrimping could be a way to make, or supplement, a living for many who either pulled shrimp from the sea, sold it raw at the dock or the market, or cooked from a tray or pushcart on the street. Among the latter were the African American

Shrimp and grits, a Southern U.S. Lowcountry favourite.

Home-made shrimp baiting poles, Southern U.S.

shrimp vendors who sold fried shrimp from hand-pushed carts on the streets in Charleston, South Carolina. They purchased their wares from the Gullah-speaking fishermen of the 'Mosquito Fleet'. The men of the Mosquito Fleet had learned their skills as boatmen from their African ancestors, slaves who had been brought to the South Carolina Sea Islands in the 1600s to work the indigo and rice plantations there. Largely cut off from the mainland, especially after the Civil War when whites fled the islands fearing a Union invasion, the Gullah people spoke patois and created a cooking style that is a congeries of African and European techniques with flavours of the West Indies and the American South

Shrimp boats, Port Royal, South Carolina.

added in. Many of the signature dishes of the Lowcountry, including the popular shrimp and grits, have roots here. Although Gullah people still live in the area, much of the traditional culture was lost as commercialization and tourism expanded in the twentieth century.

From the end of the nineteenth century and well into the twentieth, the story of shrimp production became largely American. It was in the coastal regions of the south Atlantic and the Gulf of Mexico where the most concentrated shrimp fishing and processing occurred. The states of Louisiana, Mississippi, Florida, Georgia, Texas, Alabama and the Carolinas all played a role as shrimp grew to become a major multimillion-dollar international industry.

The process at first was slow and shrimping remained a local and small-scale business, but after the American Civil War, technology accelerated. Innovations took shrimp from a seasonal treat for local folks, or the occasional seaside holiday splurge, to a year-round main course and a fast-food restaurant staple. And for a time, the American bayou and the Lowcountry were at the centre of it all.

3
Fashion Plates: Shrimp Cocktail on Ice

Before Clarence Birdseye perfected techniques for commercially freezing food in 1924, most shrimp came from a tin can. Even after the quality of frozen foods continued to improve in the 1930s and '40s, and more Americans acquired refrigerators for storing them, many consumers actually preferred the canned product. It would not be until well after the end of the Second World War that middle-class homes in the UK and Europe also had refrigerators and freezers, so it is not surprising that the availability of frozen shrimp did not at first cause widespread excitement. In order for grocers and wholesalers to make more space in the freezer case, shrimp marketers had to convince consumers that frozen shrimp were every bit as good as canned – after they had spent years trying to convince them that canned were better than fresh. On that score, they were evidently successful. In 1941 the (American) Shrimp Canners National Advertising Association credited their aggressive marketing campaign with raising canned shrimp sales to an all-time high.

Although few today would use canned shrimp for something like a shrimp cocktail, where freshness, size and presentation are desired as much as flavour, people did not immediately see the benefits in frozen shrimp – especially

u.s. Fisheries recipe booklet for using canned shrimp, 1964.

because, early on, shrimp were frozen solid in one big block, making it nearly impossible to portion off and defrost only a few. Soon food writers began to explain how to handle frozen shrimp, and instruct people how to use them in recipes, but it would take some time before they gained the kind of popularity that canned shrimp had enjoyed for most of the twentieth century.

One thing that helped was the increase in tourism in the interwar and post-war periods. Holiday destinations in the Southern u.s. began to draw large numbers of tourists between the World Wars, and became even more popular after the Second World War ended, when automobile and air travel boomed. Part of the fun of venturing to new places was sampling the local cuisine. Restaurateurs happily obliged them. The desire for the 'tastes of the tropics' in the form of exotic fresh seafood and fruit and vegetables – wholly unlike the meat and potatoes the tourists had left behind – helped promote Southern tourism and created new customers for restaurants and suppliers alike. Smitten travellers wanted to relive their holiday experiences when they returned home. This led to the phenomenon of seafood restaurants in towns and cities hundreds of miles from the nearest shore – complete with nautical decor and even the occasional palm tree.

Before long, seafood processors looked for ways to make it easier to work with the frozen product. Once they became available, individually quick frozen shrimp became the preferred type. Frozen shrimp could be kept on hand for quick meals at home, and they also made it possible for restaurants to specialize in serving fresh seafood all year round. If anything, frozen shrimp only raised expectations for the product in terms of quality and freshness. Now, there was no excuse for shrimp to be anything less than excellent. Canned shrimp, once everyone's favourite, became a thing of the past.

Holiday postcard from Fort Meyers, Florida, mid-20th century.

A century earlier, 'King Oyster' had been by far the favourite seafood of Americans and Europeans. In fact, the U.S. was said to be in the grip of an oyster craze. It would take a concerted effort on the part of the various shrimp producers and marketers before it could even break into the canned seafood market, let alone overtake the oyster.

The first major developments along the way to the industrialization of shrimping occurred in canning, cooling and shipping technologies. Before the invention of manufactured ice, preserving perishable foods in glass jars or sealed tin cans was one of the only ways to send them to distant markets or to keep the food for future use. Techniques for preserving foods in tin cans had been improving since the beginning of the nineteenth century, and by 1840 the city of Baltimore, Maryland, near the Chesapeake Bay, was the world centre of the oyster canning business.

Shrimp fishing was still very much a local and seasonal business, dealing mostly with the fresh product, although some of the catch was dried. One obstacle encountered by the early shrimp canners was that many people had never even seen a shrimp before. Others considered them little better than insects by another name. One ex-pat described the awakening he had upon tasting them in Europe for the first time:

> I had never seen shrimps before I left America; and but for my curiosity, would as soon eat a handful of huge fleas. So, with prawns; both were new to me, and both detestable for a week or two.[1]

Although he eventually developed a taste for them, it was hardly a sure bet that others would, or that they would push aside the oyster in favour of the strange-looking newcomer. People then did not have the negative associations with canned foods that they now have, so it was not the cans that bothered them, but what was inside the cans that would prove to be off-putting.

Developments that would profoundly redraw the contours of the American seafood business were on the horizon, however. Towards the end of the nineteenth century, with the expansion of the manufactured ice business and new railroad connections between Mobile, Alabama, and New Orleans, Louisiana, in 1870, the entire gulf region began to open up to the possibility of collecting the refrigerated shrimp from ports all along the coast, processing it at central locations and then shipping it by rail across the u.s. and beyond.

It was still very much an open question whether there would be a demand for canned shrimp. And it had required no small amount of imagination, or funds, to see the potential market for the product in the first place. Enter the Dunbar family of Louisiana, and the family scion, George. After returning from France, where his father had sent him to wait out the American Civil War, young George arrived home with an expensive education in canning fruits and fancy syrups. With his brother Francis, he set up a floating oyster and shrimp cannery in 1867. Soon, the newly established rail connections allowed them to move permanently to New Orleans. Once settled there, they set about purchasing the catch from the shrimp fishermen who worked up and down the Gulf Coast. They had it packed in ice and delivered directly to their canning works, via train, for processing.

Owing to oxidation, canned shrimp turned an unappetizing shade of black in a matter of weeks. This discolouration quickly turned off consumers, who, aside from disliking the appearance, also feared the product was contaminated or spoiled. Success in shrimp canning depended on finding a way to prevent this from happening. In 1876 the Dunbars received a patent for their idea of packing the cooked shrimp into cotton muslin bags before putting them into the cans. This idea may have belonged to Mrs Dunbar, George's wife, whose name, it should be noted, does not appear on the patent.[2] Later cans were coated with lacquers which prevented contact between the metal interior and shrimp, reducing the possibility of discolouration. Other methods were tried, including lining cans with wooden veneers or paper. But it was this first breakthrough of using cheap fabric bags that kept the shrimp in a suitable condition and persuaded enough consumers to begin purchasing large quantities of canned shrimp.

The Dunbars' next move was another expansion, this time to Biloxi, Mississippi, the home of an already thriving boat-building and shrimping industry. There they partnered with two ambitious local businessmen and formed the Biloxi Canning Company in 1884. Almost all of the shrimp along the gulf intended for canning was now quickly preserved

Dunbar's Canned Shrimp advertising trade card, early 20th century.

in ice, packed in sawdust for insulation and sent by train to the canning works in either New Orleans or Biloxi (these were the only two shrimp canning locations in the u.s.). At the shipyards there, the canneries constructed their own fleet of 'Biloxi schooners'. They also added an ice manufacturing plant in order to have control over the entire process and to maximize profits. They employed thousands in the shrimp works, many of whom lived in the unheated shotgun-style factory housing built for the migrant worker families who came down from Baltimore when oyster work was slack. Until u.s. labour laws put an end to it, workers

Immigrant workers in Biloxi, Mississippi, photographed by social worker Lewis Hine, 1908.

were paid with 'shrimp nickels' in lieu of actual currency. They could purchase food and other supplies with the shrimp nickels – which were usable only in the factory-owned company store.

The Biloxi Canning Company filled train cars full of canned shrimp and oysters and shipped their products across the u.s. and to parts of Europe and the uk, where they delivered more than five hundred cases of shrimp to one firm alone in 1895. By 1902 Biloxi was operating twelve canneries, with a catch of 4,424,000 lb of shrimp (and close to 6 million lb of oysters) per year.[3] The men who owned these canneries also owned the fishing fleets, controlled the majority of the yearly catch and owned the factories where the shrimp catch was processed, the housing where the workers lived and the store where they bought their groceries. The small Gulf Coast town's population had nearly quadrupled since the early 1880s, and it was proclaimed the Seafood Capital of the World.

Much of that success had depended on the labour of southern European immigrants, including their very young children, who had begun to arrive in Biloxi via railroad boxcars during the winter of 1890.

The shrimp processors were proactive in marketing their products, and sometimes combined the lure of their scenic location with the delights of their local harvest at shrimp luncheons and other such promotional events. In appealing to the consumers they considered to be 'shrimp illiterates', marketers had several options. One sure way was to get the product into the customer's mouth via the free sample. At the National Canners Association annual meeting in Louisville, Kentucky, in 1922, the enterprising gentleman who did double duty as both Mayor of Biloxi and the Secretary of the Southern Canners Association spearheaded a wildly successful 'shrimp drive', at which an estimated 20,000 visitors enjoyed a taste of shrimp cocktail, many for the first time.[4]

Children shrimp pickers, Biloxi, Mississippi, photographed by Lewis Hine, c. 1908.

Marketers made use of opinion pieces planted in newspapers and extolled the virtues of canned shrimp to 'inland dwellers' who would find it 'much to their advantage' to start using it frequently. Readers were advised that the benefits of this 'brain food' were numerous, and the canned variety meant it was always 'ready for use' in a 'creamed or à la King dish' or in a salad 'as a foundation and garnish'.[5]

Scores of canned shrimp recipes ran in local newspapers. Many were reprinted in multiple outlets, but the recipes were not always the most inspired concoctions. In addition to such gems as 'buttered shrimps', which was nothing more than canned shrimp warmed through in melted butter, and the innumerable shrimp salads which amounted to shrimp combined with mayonnaise, there was one dish that seemed to have unending appeal as the favourite of the college or university girl: the 'shrimp wiggle'. Essentially, it consisted of canned shrimp, heated in a white sauce, with the addition of canned (naturally) petits pois. It supposedly gained its name from the way the shrimp wiggled when tossed into the hot pan. The hallmark of the dish was that it was meant to display the independence of the New Woman, for whom domestic servants were unnecessary. For the dish to be truly successful, however, it was best served from her own silver chafing dish. How much shrimp wiggle was actually cooked and served this way is unknown, but the recipe appeared over and over again throughout the first decades of the twentieth century.

In addition to the chafing dish, successfully serving and enjoying shrimp also required other paraphernalia for the table – shrimp forks and cocktail icers, scallop-shaped trays with attached saucers (and, later, toothpick holders) and crystal or cut-glass shrimp bowls all began to appear. Just as the oyster had demanded the appropriate compartmented serving plate, shrimp also came with a retinue, and that included rules of etiquette. Eating shrimp, particularly larger ones, in public could be especially vexing, as they could be unwieldy, slippery and incompletely shelled, making dinner parties and other social engagements more fraught and messy than necessary.

The rise in shrimp's popularity also coincided with a turn towards a much lighter eating style than had been in fashion throughout most of the nineteenth century. The multi-course spreads of the Victorian era were giving way to lighter fare, with an emphasis on salads and fewer dishes overall. With changing fashions in clothing, especially the corset-less dresses after the end of the First World War, a new interest in slimming had arrived.

No dish is more representative of the jazz age, or has had such universal appeal, than the shrimp cocktail. It was easy and elegant and modern in its lightness. And although it was thoroughly of an age and a time – of canned shrimp, iceboxes, fiddly salads dressed in ketchup and served in cut-glass coupes and eaten with oyster forks – it has managed to transcend its era and become one of the few truly timeless dishes still enjoyed today.

Several myths circulate about the name 'cocktail'. Some suggest that it was an American appellation that came about as a result of Prohibition in 1918, which forbade the sale of alcohol, thereby giving resourceful u.s. hostesses a new use for their cocktail glassware. The facts do not support this theory, however. As early as 1908, the *Dallas Morning News* carried an advertisement in which a restaurant featured shrimp cocktail as part of the bill of fare. The word 'cocktail' had been in general use for at least a century by then and could mean an alcoholic beverage, but it was also used to describe a fruit melange. Similarly, the oyster, and its bivalve cousin the clam, in cocktail dress, were already popular appetizers or first courses by the end of the nineteenth century and appeared on menus ranging from the humblest luncheonette to grand hotel restaurants.

Magazines and newspapers reprinted the recipe countless times. With instructions that come down to placing a cupful of spiced ketchup in the vicinity of some cold shrimp, the notion of assigning an inventor seems a tad overblown. A very early printed recipe for 'Shrimp Cocktail' appeared in the *San Jose Mercury* (California) on 15 October 1912, and was reprinted elsewhere, but it seems as likely to have been a promotion for a product called Burnett's Color Paste. Mayonnaise – tinted to a pale green – covered the mound of canned shrimp, which sat aboard individual lettuce-lined serving glasses. The recipe did not specify amounts for any ingredients and it simply called for cleaning fresh shrimp and chilling them before use. The cook was instructed to season the shrimp with salt, paprika and chilli sauce and garnish the whole thing with celery tips.

More iconic recipes appeared featuring a tomato-based dressing, usually ketchup but sometimes chilli sauce, with lemon and an element of heat provided by horseradish and cayenne pepper. The American-style cocktail was also a popular export. In the UK, this basic formula is often altered into what is known as Marie Rose sauce with the addition of mayonnaise or salad cream. There, when the recipe appeared, foreign ingredients such as Tabasco sauce were explained to readers.

For many, the shrimp cocktail was a powerful symbol of success and the good life, and even acculturation. Food writer Julia Moskin remembered how her grandmother, a successful woman in New York City's garment business, followed Jewish dietary laws and kept kosher every other day of the year but for Thanksgiving, when she served shrimp cocktails before the main course. The shrimp cocktail symbolized for her, a Russian immigrant, everything she had achieved, and was

Classic shrimp cocktail with hot sauce and lemon.

'the ultimate expression of American wealth and luxury'.[6] A freeze-dried version even accompanied American astronauts into space, quickly becoming a favourite at the 'final frontier'.

As much as some people would like to declare that it has had its day, it seems that the shrimp cocktail just cannot be surpassed. It is impervious to change. For all the proclamations about its being passé and a tired retro standby, and something that is only eaten now with a large shrimp-forkful of irony, it turns up on every celebrity chef's dossier at some point. The most famous chefs in the world eventually present recipes for it. They may give it some sort of personal twist, or try to reinvent it, but even they can never stray too far from the template or it is no longer reliably a shrimp cocktail. It has been dressed up with all manner of folderol. Avocado, chipotle peppers, wasabi, pomegranates, pulverized nuts, sriracha – all have been tried and, ultimately, rejected. It is hard to improve on a classic.

No matter how often it is maligned as a cliché and a bore, it continues to appear – usually, it must be said, to something like delight – on banquet spreads, at cocktail parties and intimate dinners for two, in cookbooks and on celebrity food shows and, if you are fortunate, at a table near you.

4

Powder and Paste
and a Sense of Place

In much of the world, cheese-laced snacks reign supreme – chips, crisps, crackers, sauces, dips, breads, pretzels and so on offer bright orange helpings of cheese-like flavour. But a large part of the world finds cheese – and cheesy aromas – repellent. To satisfy the apparently universal hunger for something salty and crunchy (and usually devoid of all nourishment), these cultures have at their disposal an equally addictive and adaptive flavouring that can also be baked in, sprinkled on or stirred into virtually any carbohydrate-based substrate made to hold still long enough for it to stick. Shrimp or prawn flavours give a salty, savoury burst to a huge array of snack foods in many of the world's cuisines. Even where other flavourings, such as cheese or chilli spices, are also popular, shrimp-flavoured crackers, crisps and other crunchy items have found a huge audience of admirers.

Among the best known are the widely available shrimp crackers. Originally from Indonesia, they are called *krupuk udang*, and are typically served as appetizers or as accompaniments to restaurant fare. They are found in Asian groceries and supermarkets, and of course, with the ease of online shopping, a whole variety of shapes and sizes can be ordered and delivered almost everywhere. Some easy-to-find brands come from Thailand, Malaysia, Taiwan, China, Japan, South Korea and Indonesia. In Europe, they gained popularity first in the Netherlands (where they are known as *kroepoek*), because of that country's colonial history with Indonesia. In general, they are crispy and deep fried (although some are baked) – a little bit salty and sweet. The cracker base itself is usually made either from tapioca or wheat starch, or sometimes potato, and contains oil and shrimp paste, although there are some artificially flavoured ones now available. The familiar flavour varies in intensity and may not be immediately identifiable as shrimp. Despite the sometimes vaguely threatening-looking shrimp on the outside of the package, they tend to be rather mild. They are typically a pale straw-colour, but some, especially Chinese varieties, are pastel-coloured. The snacks can be purchased already cooked, in cellophane bags and in cardboard tubes for a quick nibble. They are also available uncooked and ready to be deep fried at home. Another popular shrimp-flavoured snack, especially in Thailand (but it is catching on elsewhere), is the practice of eating packaged noodle soup

Spicy shrimp crackers.

Japanese shrimp crackers and wafers.

– but not in the traditional sense of a bowl of steaming broth. Rather, the snacking fashion is to break the noodle cake into pieces, mix it with the foil packet of soup mix, and eat it that way in all its salty, shrimpy glory. Dilution with water is neither required nor desired.

Two of the great loves of many in Western societies – deep-fried potato snacks and shrimp cocktail – are joined in a hot pink bag of shame in an inspired (if only symbolic) marriage in the famous Walkers (and several pretenders') prawn-cocktail-flavoured crisps. The shrimp flavour is merely illusory. They are entirely free of any crustacean matter whatsoever, and it is only the tomato Marie Rose-sauce flavouring which gives the snack its suggestion of prawniness. Nevertheless, some people have been convinced that the product contains the shellfish. According to the FAQ list on the Leicester-based snack company's website, the crisps 'do not use real prawns as they would carry an allergy risk'. On

Crumbled noodle-soup mix is a favourite snack.

the other hand, the prawn-cocktail flavour does contain real tomatoes – a fact which would seem to leave tomato-allergy sufferers in a bit of a fix. The 'prawn cocktail flavour' turns out to be not only a misnomer, but an outlier. It is the taste of shrimp, or more to the point the taste miracle of umami that shrimp deliver – in the form of shrimp paste, powder and sauce – that is sought when shrimp-flavoured snacks are craved. This is why it makes such a welcome and frequent appearance in snack foods and instant ramen noodle packets found in corner shops and student housing from Asia to North America and all points in between. Shrimp flavour, especially in its concentrated form, is one of nature's edible gifts.

What cheese and shrimp share, aside from saltiness, is umami or the taste of savouriness, or meatiness – even a signal to the brain and gut that protein will be involved in the meal. It has been called the 'fifth flavour', joining with the quartet of better-known receptors more familiar to Western tastes: sour, salty, bitter and sweet. It has been popular in Asian cuisines for centuries, but only in the last several decades has it been recognized by American and European consumers and chefs who now look for ways to impart umami through foods such as Parmesan cheese, dried tomatoes, anchovies and mushrooms. It is less a new discovery and more of a rediscovery in Western cuisines, as it was favoured by the Greeks and Romans in their fish sauce *garum*, which has been unfairly maligned, and which was apparently made, and enjoyed, by millions of citizens for hundreds of years.[1]

It would be selling shrimp flavour much too short to limit it to the realm of junk food, because although it has had success there, it has also played a larger and more important role in serious cuisine, in both its fresh whole form and in its transformed states as a liquid, a paste or in its dried version, whole or ground into a powder. People long ago discovered that dried shrimp can be preserved and carried further than fresh,

Thai tom yam soup.

both geographically and also in flavour. Shrimp paste and dried shrimp can create the sense that there is more protein in a meal than there is in reality, an important consideration when diets are composed mainly of carbohydrate-rich foods.

First used in Southeast Asia in the fifteenth century, the best shrimp paste today is still made in small quantities, by hand, by what are essentially small-scale home-producers. It takes about 10 kg (22 lb) of shrimp to make 1 kg (2 lb) of the best artisanal paste.[2] But it is a threatened craft, as factory farming lowers the quality of the shrimp, and younger generations seem less concerned with maintaining the fastidious attention to details that preoccupied their parents and grandparents.

In the nineteenth century, Chinese migrants to the West Coast of the U.S. built a thriving export business drying shrimp and sending it back to China. This was one of the first large-scale commercial shrimp industries in the U.S., but it was short-lived, the victim of anti-Chinese sentiments and

Shrimp paste, an essential ingredient in Thai and Malaysian cuisine.

fears of overfishing and economic competition that came to a head with legislation that closed the industry down.

Dried shrimp are still widely used in many parts of the world as a snack, but also as a flavouring component. They can be ground into a paste, or reconstituted with water for soups or stews. In one West African nation, the Republic of Cameroon, the shrimp are unequalled. In fact, the name of the country itself comes from the Portuguese word for them: *camarõe*. The Cameroonian national dish of *ndolé* combines peanuts, bitter greens and cooked shrimp, and many recipes call for dried shrimp to be added to the gravy to create a more complex flavour.

Shrimp dishes are often reserved for celebrations, to show hospitality and to express love, so it may be why some are so closely entwined with a place or with the experience of a place. The Brazilian festival food *caruru* is an enduring dish that reaffirms bonds among family and friends and would be incomplete without shrimp. The flavour of shrimp can create powerful ties with a precise place on the map, but at the same time it can be of no particular place, or every place.

There may be no better example of how a shrimp dish has served as a bridge between cultures than in the classic of Japanese cuisine, and now a worldwide favourite, *ebi tempura* (shrimp tempura). Surrounded by water, the Japanese are no strangers to seafood. Aside from tempura, they have made other famous contributions to shrimp cuisine. One notable contribution that is seldom encountered at the neighbourhood sushi joint is the *odori ebi* – 'dancing shrimp' – so-called because it is eaten while still alive and moving (giving the impression of being mid-dance). It takes skill to properly prepare and it is expensive, which is part of the allure. To serve, the head and shell are removed and then it is subdued in *sake* and soy sauce and taken in one quick wriggly bite. While it may

The Brazilian festival food *caruru*.

Shrimp ceviche marries shrimp and tropical flavours in a cool salad.

sound extreme, it pays to remember that oysters and clams, cooled on ice, doused in lemon and hot pepper sauce, and slurped up in great multitudes, do not completely shed their own mortal coil until the moment they are detached from the half-shell on which they are so often served.

But to return to *ebi tempura* – batter-coated, deep-fried shrimp – its name, its ingredients and its technique all reveal its mixed heritage. When Jesuit missionaries arrived in Japan after 1549, they had to work hard to overcome the bad impression left behind by earlier compatriots. The Japanese had been less than impressed by their previous European guests, whom they found ill-mannered and crude. The missionaries ended up getting themselves thrown out anyway, along with all other Westerners (with the exception of a few Dutch traders) in 1638. This time, the Japanese believed the Jesuits had overstepped politically, and they feared an invasion by the Spanish. Foreigners were barred for more than two centuries after that. Although the Japanese sent the missionaries packing, they held on to their recipe for the batter-fried shrimp they ate at their Embertide 'fish meals'. In the Catholic calendar, Embertide occurs four times each year, or, in Latin, *quatour tempora*. The Japanese thought they could improve on the recipe, though, and they did. They changed the oil, using a lighter blend. They

Shrimp tempura is one of Japan's great contributions to world cuisine.

experimented with temperatures. They thinned the batter. They refined the frying technique. They renamed it *ebi tempura* – shrimp tempura. It has become one of the most renowned dishes in the world and deservedly so. And it is an excellent example of a fusion of flavours and techniques that arrives at something altogether new.[3] While it is of two places originally, and then one, it has become so universally loved and eaten that it has almost transcended nationality. Shrimp tempura can now be eaten almost anywhere in the world. It is the dish that is served to finicky toddlers and grandparents because it does not seem too 'foreign' or strange.

A more recent addition to the Japanese shrimp repertoire, another fusion of Eastern and Western flavours and techniques, can be found in McDonald's' *ebi* Filet-O sandwich, available in Japan (and found in some other Asian markets, where it is known as the Shrimp Burger). Only time will tell if it will have the same sort of impact *ebi tempura* has had.

5
Jumbo Shrimp and Other Tidbits: Shrimp in Art, Literature and Society

The American sitcom *Seinfeld*, famously 'about nothing', was actually a comedy of manners which found much of its humour in a critique of the social mores of *fin de siècle* middle-class urbanites.[1] The season eight episode 'The Comeback', which first aired in the U.S. on 30 January 1997, finds the misanthropic character George in a workplace conference room, seated in front of a large bowl of shrimp. He is barely participating in the meeting as he stuffs shrimp in his mouth with both hands. As George continues to gorge on the catered shrimp, a colleague remarks, 'Hey, George, the ocean called, they're running out of shrimp,' and the entire room erupts in laughter. Flummoxed, George cannot think of an appropriate response until much later. When he eventually does, he must take a plane halfway across the country to personally deliver the unfortunate rejoinder: 'Oh, yeah, well the "Jerk Store" called. They're running out of you!' Things go from bad to worse for George from there, and the nonsense insult 'jerk store' entered the lexicon.

George is in most ways an unlikeable character, perennially victimized in his own mind. What nonetheless makes him a relatable everyman is that viewers often can identify with his predicaments. Here he has made an enormous fool of himself and behaves unforgivably, although his anger, and his insistence on retaliation, seem somewhat disproportionate to the blow he received. In fact, this character's unbridled appetite has caused him social embarrassment in other episodes, yet it is the particular act of getting caught with his hand deep in the shrimp bowl – and being publicly shamed for it – that has left him socially paralysed and unable to defend himself verbally.

By the late 1990s, the public had been exposed to over forty years of persuasion aimed at convincing consumers, through visual demonstrations of veritable mountains of shrimp, ecstatic salivating diners, lascivious utterances, endless shrimp fests, bottomless shrimp bowls, all-you-can-eat shrimp buffets, shrimp-a-paloozas and so on, that helpless surrender was a rational response to the premise of eating one's weight in shrimp, and that this behaviour was both natural and to be expected. Entire marketing campaigns, including some created for the largest international seafood restaurant chain, Red Lobster, but many others too, were built around the idea that shrimp itself promotes a loss of self-control, and that it is permissible to indulge freely, in part, because the supply is boundless. The message to consumers, for the majority of that time, was that eating shrimp presented a no-holds-barred opportunity for unchecked self-gratification.

Long touted as a healthful food for dieters, and as a low-fat, low-calorie opportunity to abandon caution in the 1980s, by the 1990s shrimp's high cholesterol count was suddenly under scrutiny. Shellfish in general started to seem suspect. At the same time, repeated dire warnings about overfishing, environmental destruction, damage to the ecosystem, ravages to the ocean floor, human rights violations and violent conflicts over territory and fishing rights made the cocktail hour an ethical dilemma.

When his behaviour is considered against the cultural subtext, George's social transgression and his painful 'outing' can be read as a skewering of the manufactured 'shrimp lust' that informed it. Much of George's anger, and the uncomfortable humour that arises from it, stems from the fact that he has been betrayed and publicly ridiculed for exhibiting the very behaviour that he has been encouraged to embrace at every turn; behaviour he has been conditioned to believe is not only normal, but expected. As so often happens with George, somebody changed the rules, and he was the last to know. Twenty years on, many viewers can still probably identify all too well with George – who, after all, was just a guy standing in front of the free shrimp plate, eating far too many, unable to stop, wondering why, yet overjoyed to be alone with it, and wishing no one was watching.

It appears there is a historical tendency for people to make fools of themselves over free, or at least abundant, shrimp. One nineteenth-century British writer described a kind of shrimp-induced reverie, and expressed the notion that 'many men's sweetest memories are connected with shrimps.'[2] The famed nineteenth-century journalist James Greenwood, better known for exposing London's seamy underbelly, described a day trip to Gravesend in nearby Kent. The main attraction, for the many Londoners who flocked there, was the feast 'never yet known to fail' – 'the ninepenny shrimp tea'. Greenwood, the famed 'muckraker', claimed to have witnessed a family of 'true shrimp lovers' devouring the objects of their affection, 'armour and all'. In so doing, he wrote, they had produced 'such a munching' it sounded as if they were breaking up 'match-wood'. The patriarch, whose waistcoat was 'abundantly festooned with legs and scales', declined when offered another cup of tea, but did request another saucer-full of the plump shrimp he referred to as 'big-uns'. Finishing that, and with time to spare before the return train, he crunched through yet another serving.[3]

Far from being a new obsession, shrimp, at least as a motif, have intrigued people for thousands of years. One of the earliest examples of shrimp serving as an inspiration for artistic expression is in a stunning piece of jewellery made by the Moche people of Peru sometime during the third to fifth century CE, now on display at the Metropolitan Museum of Art in New York. The elegant nose ornament is made of silver and depicts two realistic shrimp of inlaid gold, detailed with stone. Whatever their symbolic meaning, shrimp remained an important design element in the early American civilizations. One thousand years later, in a rapidly unravelling attempt to forestall disaster at the hands of the Spanish invaders, the Aztec chief Moctezuma offered Hernán Cortés 'two collars of shells' of the type which were held in high esteem among his own people.[4] What was far more pleasing

Gold and silver nose ornament with shrimp, Moche (*Loma Negra*), Peru, 390–450 CE.

to the Spaniard's eyes, however, was that 'from each of the collars hung eight golden shrimps a span long, and executed with great perfection'. The Meso-American goldsmiths were master craftsmen. Unfortunately, the conquistadores in general had little interest in Aztec aesthetics and symbolism, and likely soon melted down the priceless gifts. The Aztecs were not a literate culture, so there is no written record to explain what the shrimp might have meant, but they used animals in their zodiac and in other representations, and this gift was among the last in a procession that had already included many 'extravagant' offerings such as a Spanish helmet returned to its owner filled to the rim with gold dust, and jewellery made of precious metals and encrusted with emeralds.

In Asian cultures, stretching well into the past, the shrimp has been considered a symbol of luck and longevity. Because it sheds its shell in the moulting process, and seemingly re-starts life afresh, it is also used as a signifier of rebirth or renewal. In Japan, *ebi* (it means both shrimp and lobster) designs are incorporated into samurai armour for good luck; they are used in the family crests known as *mon*, and frequently appear as elements in textile design, ceramics and other fine arts such as woodcut prints. In the nineteenth century, the landscape painter and printmaker Hiroshige achieved fame and cemented his place as an enduring influence for generations of artists in the East and West. His images of flowers and animals and, of course, shrimp and crayfish, which he painted in the 1830s and '40s, are iconic.

The twentieth-century Chinese painter Qi Baishi is regarded as the greatest shrimp painter in history for his hundreds of highly esteemed and valued watercolours that capture the transparency of the body of the shrimp – said to be one of the most difficult to render of all nature's subjects. Today, his images, or close copies of them, are used widely

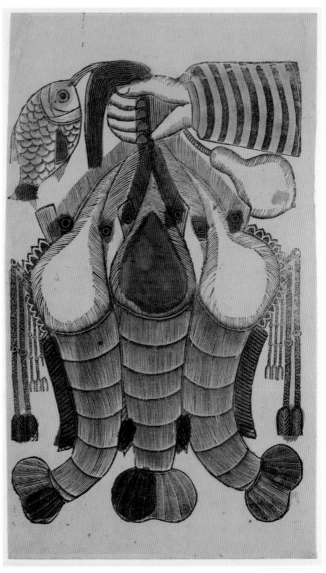

Hand with Freshwater Shrimps, 19th century, woodcut, Bengal.

Hiroshige (1797–1858), woodblock print.

on such things as ceramics, paper goods, cross-stitch kits, learning-to-paint books and also paper scrolls, a testament to how much Qi Baishi's paintings are loved.

European artists have also embraced the culture of the shrimp and this is often manifested in subjects that combine it with themes close to the heart of the Enlightenment project – technology, childhood and a love of nature. People from the poorer classes frequently procured or sold shrimp as part of their livelihood, and William Hogarth's mid-eighteenth-century 'flesh and blood' painting of *The Shrimp Girl* captures a young woman, full of high spirits, engaged in this sort of street peddling, which became part of the character of city life well into the Victorian era. Images of children splashing in the surf and collecting shrimp in hand-held nets appeared throughout the nineteenth and early twentieth centuries in fine art, such as in the Impressionist paintings of Dorothea Sharp, and in more commercial work featured in engravings and photographs in newspapers and magazines.

Shrimps!

Engrav'd from an Original Sketch in Oil by Hogarth, in the Possession of M.ʳˢ Hogarth.

Publish'd March 4ᵗ, 1782 by Jane Hogarth & R.ᵈ Livesay Leicester Fields.

Francesco Bartolozzi after William Hogarth, *The Shrimp Girl, c.* 1785.

Leisure and tourism activities also blossomed in the nineteenth century and representations of the dual aspect of the shrimp economy, as both a means of earning a living and as a source of pleasure travel, abounded. Gossip columns reported tirelessly about celebrities dining on shrimp and champagne after their morning swims at international beach resorts. Postcards and other memorabilia depicted rows of shrimp boats at dock, heaped plates of cooked shrimp, freshly caught shrimp in nets or, as in one popular card that was adapted for virtually any locale from Blackpool to Atlantic City, an illustration of the holiday destination ringed with a wreath of glossy embossed pink-shelled shrimp.

In present-day popular culture, shrimp adorn everything from seaside holiday kitsch to the Sanrio company's 'Hello Kitty' trinkets, to fine art reproductions and all sorts of products in between, including stuffed bed pillows, children's plush toys and Christmas tree ornaments. An anthropomorphized prawn, Pepe, featured in The Muppets'

Dorothea Sharp (1874–1955), *At the Seaside*.

line-up in films including *Muppets from Space* (1999), and has penned his own biography, *It's Hard Out Here for a Shrimp*. A manga-style mascot is depicted on the wrapper of the shrimp-mayonnaise-flavoured variety of the Japanese snack food Yaokin Umaibo Sticks, and the computer-generated superhero shrimp Yijiro defends the small and weak in the Nickelodeon Network's serial *Kung Fu Panda* in the episode 'The Way of the Prawn'.

Feminine fashion, too, has adopted the curly pale-pink icon as its own. It has appeared as a design motif and colour-way in fabrics, and as a flattering hue for nail lacquer, lipstick, rouge and face powder in 'the shade known as pale shrimp', recommended especially for the 'woman whose pallor is a trouble to her'.[5] Its all-time popularity seems to have peaked in the 1920s, but it makes periodic comebacks. In 2014 the breakout UK fashion company Shrimps caught international attention for its surreal-coloured faux fur coats. Called '*the* name to wear' that year (and in subsequent ones as well), its identity and logo derive from the 'sweet, very English pet

Ubiquitous holiday postcard, this one from the resort town of Blackpool, UK.

Japanese shrimp-mayonnaise-flavour snack with anime-style package art.

name for a tiny blonde poppet' given to its design head, the London College of Fashion graduate Hannah Weiland, as a child.[6]

The sex appeal of the saucy shrimp should not be under-estimated. In an undated postcard illustration from the first part of the twentieth century, a glamorous shrimp with the

Shrimp-shaped, banana-flavoured sweets.

head of a woman and the body of a crustacean appears dressed as a charming young girl, replete with pink gown and matching parasol, as she strolls along a boardwalk. In the 1890s the internationally famous actress 'the divine' Sarah Bernhardt was rumoured to rely on shrimps and raw eggs to maintain her beauty. This was a story she apparently denied, but who is really to say? (It was a beauty secret, after all.) Even today shrimp are regularly promoted as a pick-me-up for a low mood, a diet boost and an aphrodisiac, owing, it is said, to their high levels of zinc.

The linking of shellfish and sex has an ancient history, however.[7] Ancient Greek poets and playwrights used sea creatures to make obscene jokes and double entendres about the sexual organs, and sexuality in general. Shrimp often figure in many works as stand-ins, because of their colour and form, for the male genitalia, for the obvious entertainment value.

The word itself, of course, rhymes with 'imp', and the imagined characteristic of the creature as a clown or object

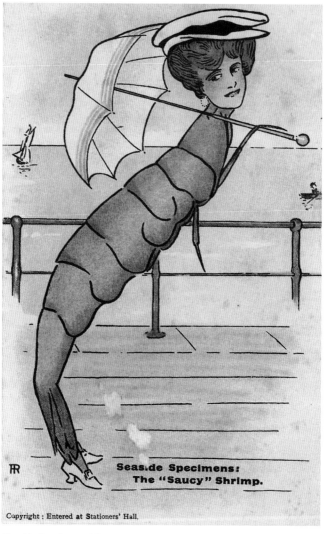

Seaside Specimens:
The "Saucy" Shrimp.

'Seaside Specimens: The "Saucy" Shrimp', early 20th-century British postcard.

I was an impudent imp
Who invited an over-cooked shrimp
  To a slide on the ice,
  As the weather was nice.
Next day the shrimp walked with a limp.

Edmund Dulac, 'I is for Imp', from *Lyrics Pathetic and Humorous from A to Z* (1908).

of amusement is often emphasized, especially in artwork and rhymes meant for children, and in whimsical bits of nonsense such as the 1844 poem 'Song of the Shellfish: The Shrimp', wherein a devilish fellow, 'red as satanical imp', asks, 'What son of the sea can vie with me, the scampering, scavenger shrimp?' This playful and athletic aspect has been employed for the naming of racehorses and yachts, and sportsmen, such as one 'chubby fellow' who caused 'much amusement' – a baseball utility infielder named 'Shrimp' Miller, who played with the team the New Yorks in 1901.[8] It was also the name given to a dangerous little juvenile delinquent, a cartoon figure called Shrimp Flynn, in the comic strip 'U.S. Boys' in the 1910s.[9]

While it can be used in a jovial or flirtatious manner for men or women, as an insult it is almost always directed towards men. This may be linked to the association of the phallus with the shrimp, or because the shrimp itself, being small, weak and a colour typically associated with babies and young girls, has qualities that are in direct opposition to the cherished traits of masculinity in Western culture. According to the linguist Anatoly Liberman, however, although it may sound like a metaphor 'when we call someone small and unimportant a shrimp', the word was first used to 'designate dwarfs'. It was only later, he argues, that it 'transferred to the animal in an undocumented process'. When the word began to appear in English in the 'late Middle period' it meant 'a dwarfish creature'.[10] One of the greatest writers of insults of all time, William Shakespeare, used the word in this sense at least once. In *Henry VI, Part I* the Countess of Auvergne sizes up, and cuts to size, her enemy Lord Talbot, Earl of Shrewsbury, with the following line: 'Alas, this is a child, a silly dwarf! It cannot be this weak and writhled shrimp should strike such terror to his enemies.' (II.3) It is the modern, not the seventeenth-century, audience who hears 'shrimp' and thinks not 'little man' but 'hors d'oeuvre'.

Either way, the word itself is often used to emasculate. This has given rise to a genre of humour in which a smallish man is conflated with the sea creature. In one seaside souvenir postcard a woman calls for her daughter's shrimp net so that she may rescue her diminutive husband who has fallen into the sea. In another, a physically mismatched touring couple ask an innkeeper if she 'serves shrimps with tea'. So, as much as it could be a slightly suggestive or overtly little-girlish tag for a woman, or a gently teasing nickname for men who were obviously manly enough to defy it, it could also have a crueller side. At times, it has also been meant as a sharp rebuke. In calling a man a shrimp, not only is he belittled, but it is sometimes implied that he has been the victim of a castrating woman. An outraged group of alimony-payers in the 1920s formed a men's self-help group, declaring that 'all that a woman finds it necessary to do nowadays is bring a big charge against a man' and he will fold. They concluded that 'men as a class are a bunch of gelatine-spined shrimps.' In a 1922 torn-from-the-headlines scandal, a 'decided brunette with large, liquid black eyes' sued her wealthy 'daddy long legs' in a sensational trial and demanded $100,000 from the fellow, whom she publicly called a 'villain' and a 'shrimp' for a 'breach of promise' after their apparent quid pro quo agreement went bad. Sometimes the shrimp gets the last laugh, though. In 1914 the *New York Times* ran a short and humorous piece entitled 'Love and the Professor', on the subject of eugenics. As evidence for the 'scientific' premise at its core – that 'man is attracted by beauty and woman by strength' was no match for the 'mystery' which lurked in the human heart – it offered the example of a beautiful girl named Evelyn, who passed right by a 'six-foot Samson', and chose instead an 'anaemic little shrimp'.

Whether it is said with contempt, or as a kind of playful jabbing, it is not likely that too many people enjoy being called 'shrimp' with all that it implies. But it is unlikely that any group has suffered more indignity by comparison to the lowly crustacean than the 'small for their age' prepubescent

Postcard, mid-20th century, UK.

boys' choir unfortunately saddled with the name 'The Singing "Shrimps"'. Billed as a 'choir group from the slums', the twelve-year-old boys from London with the 'silvery voices' were so named because, according to one writer, they 'are so little people who see them call them the "shrimps"'. Dressed in travelling suits of 'picturesque Mary blue smocks, blue sandals, and black mortarboards with blue tassels', they toured the English-speaking world performing Handel, Bach and folk songs, as well as staging 'little things such as "Widdicombe Fair"'. As the choir director confessed, 'any little ragged, broken nailed, tousled lad who dares come off the streets to endure its spartan regime will find himself turned inside out.'[11]

6
All We Can Eat:
The High Cost of
Cheap Shrimp

The first petroleum-powered shrimp boat cast off from San Fernandina, Florida, in 1902. The petroleum age would, of course, profoundly affect shrimp fishing. But it was the motorized otter trawl, introduced into the Gulf of Mexico in 1917, which could stay open when dragged along the sea bottom, that dramatically increased the catch, especially in the newly discovered deep-sea shrimping areas. The otter trawl mostly replaced the age-old, hand-cast seine nets and truly revolutionized the shrimp business. At the same time, this new method did the most violence to the oyster industry, which until that time had ruled the waters and commanded the palates of the public. It also changed the character of shrimping, from a local, small-scale family business to an international one of big ships and big money; it turned shrimp into the world's most popular seafood.[1]

Later, deep-ocean fishing led to new problems, with environmental concerns taking prominence. Where people before had worried about seasonal shortages, now new fears of overfishing and rampant ecological destruction took their place. Added to this were disputes about territories and labour, as well as continued racial confrontations and animosities that had marred the shrimp business from its earliest days in the U.S.[2]

All of this did nothing to abate demand, however, and it only increased through the decades of the 1980s and '90s, and even more into the twenty-first century. The growth of Thai and Chinese restaurants in the U.S. and UK, as well as

Shrimp trawler, Southern U.S., 21st century.

Worker on a modern shrimp boat.

Baskets of shrimp for sale at an Asian market.

Water treatment at a shrimp farm, Chachengsao, Thailand.

the rising middle classes in other countries, who demanded more animal protein, certainly contributed to the increase in shrimp consumption. Farm-raised shrimp was the next great boon in feeding an insatiable global appetite. Even though consumer watchdog groups issue cautions over possible fraud, human rights abuses and health and safety violations, the limitless feast goes on. Farm-raised shrimp now makes up over half of the shrimp produced around the world, with most of that coming from China, Thailand and Indonesia, followed by other countries in Asia and South America. While it is giving an economic boost to many of the poor in those countries, it is also doing harm both ecologically and in terms of human costs.[3]

Old Wine in New Bottles

The BP Deepwater Horizon oil spill of 2010 in the Gulf of Mexico resulted in the loss of eleven lives, and was the largest petroleum accident in history. When the spill and the painstaking clean-up became news, it horrified many, and as the environmental and economic issues mounted, public concerns about food safety multiplied. This crisis, which shone a light on the devastation of the gulf area and the seafood industry there, may have been the first serious wake-up call for anyone concerned about where their shrimp was coming from.

Farmed shrimp seemed to offer an alternative to overfishing, destruction of the ocean floor and other problems that accompanied deep-ocean trawling, but instead brought a new set of concerns. While the question of flavour often comes down to personal preference, with some people maintaining that there is very little difference in taste or quality among the current options, warnings of environmental and human health risks have made headlines. Reports of sick shrimp, fetid living conditions and illegal antibiotic use appear alongside those that detail extensive mangrove destruction, adulterated feed concerns and contaminated waste run-off.

In addition, lax enforcement of almost non-existent regulations, which favour the producer over the consumer in any case, mean that it is almost impossible for the average diner to know for certain where the shrimp they are eating originated.[4] As the group Oceana points out, shrimp can appear on each of the 'Best Choices, Good Alternatives and Avoid' lists designed to guide consumers' buying decisions, resulting in confusion and frustrating efforts to make responsible choices. In the course of one of their recent investigations, Oceana discovered that in some areas, close to one-third of the shrimp sold was mislabelled. The most common practices involved selling farmed shrimp labelled as 'wild caught', or omitting the country of origin, but the group also found more alarming problems, such as the occasional non-edible aquarium interloper in a bag meant for, well, eating. The bottom line is that consumers are often paying much more for something that has come straight out of a tank. This hurts reputable brokers as well as consumers.

Workers hand-sort shrimp at a Vietnamese shrimp farm.

On top of all this, other truly shocking stories began to break in the second decade of the twenty-first century. Details have come to light about extensive human rights abuses in Thailand, Bangladesh and other nations that supply the seemingly endless quantities of frozen cleaned shrimp to the multinational big buyers and processors which supply the restaurants and food franchises in the West. These stories detail the slave labour conditions in which many workers are held and the beatings, confiscated passports, theft of earnings and other nightmares experienced by others. The Associated Press followed up these stories in 2015, and indicted many of the largest food suppliers in the West for purchasing from these suppliers. Promises to 'do better' have been sworn by all parties, including governments and major processors and distributors, but only time will tell if real change occurs. Several agencies around the world have taken on the challenge of monitoring the safety and sustainability of the world's seafood. But it is a huge challenge,

Shrimp nets, Madagascar.

This image of a young shrimp worker, Manuel, in Biloxi, Mississippi, in 1911 caused an outcry over child labour.

and many consumers seem unaware or unbothered by the problems and potential risks.

Sadly, there is nothing new under the sun, especially when it comes to the human capacity to profit from another's misery. Although the world cries out against the scenes of cruelty and inhumanity inflicted on present-day workers, it seems that the first shrimp workers to experience similar conditions have already been forgotten. Almost one hundred years ago, it was the children of poor European immigrants whose fingers and feet were eaten raw by the juices in the shrimp they peeled for hours on end in unheated sheds.

Before the invention, in 1946, of the first machine that could remove the shrimp's tough shell without crushing or tearing the delicate meat inside, human hands seemed to hold the monopoly on this skill. Although it was not difficult, it required attention and sensitivity to the task. But in the early

Handbill exposing child labour in the U.S. seafood industry, photograph by Lewis Hine, 1908.

years of the twentieth century in the u.s., the undesirable and unprotected work that paid just above starvation-level wages fell to the people who had the least ability to turn it down or to fight for better conditions: children, women, African Americans and newly arrived immigrants from Southern and Eastern Europe.

Labour was cheap and the European migrants put their children to work with them in the factories. Although this was against the law, the owners turned a blind eye, and actively recruited European families and provided ramshackle shanty-row houses. Children as young as three years old worked in the oyster and shrimp-canning businesses that popped up all along the coastal southern u.s. The work of children in seafood processing compares with the coal mines and textile mills in Britain of the nineteenth century in terms of exploitation.

Peeling was miserable, if technically simple, work. The picking works were set up right near the catch at the water's

The Daly sisters, child shrimp pickers, Biloxi, Mississippi, photographed by Lewis Hine, c. 1908.

u.s. shrimp worker photographed by Lewis Hine, *c.* 1908.

edge. The stench was remarkable as the discarded shells formed massive piles that rotted in the sun. None of the canneries had heat and the shrimp seasons were in February and March and then again in September into October. Work began at 3.30 a.m. most days and even though the temperature could climb quite high by midday, it was cold enough before the sun rose to require layers of clothing to keep warm. The arriving shrimp were packed in ice, and the workers had their hands and arms plunged into it the whole time they were working. Women and children stuffed their clothing with newspaper as insulation against the cold. Once the paper became wet it was worse than useless.

And it was harsh work. Each picker had a tin pail that held 10 lb of peeled shrimp and they filled and emptied it many times during the day, their wages dependent on the number of pounds they shelled. After the first round of shelling, the worker then picked through the batch again, carefully sifting through to make sure no bits of shell or grit were mixed in with the shrimp meat. In addition to the long hours of standing and doing the same mechanical task over and over again, the high acid content of shrimp shells burned the skin of the workers. It was so damaging that it ate through shoe leather, and any of the children who actually had shoes in the first place had only ragged ones that exposed their feet. Children's skin was particularly susceptible to damage because it was more fragile than that of adults. Workers soaked their hands in alum at night in an attempt to toughen the skin in preparation for the next day's work. Burns and open sores resulted from the constant exposure and most workers could endure only a few hours before the discomfort forced them to stop work for the day.

Lewis Hine was a pioneering American social worker who brought the lives of these children to public light through his powerful photographs and reporting. Eventually, the u.s. practices were reformed, and labour for children under twelve was outlawed in 1908, although abuses went on nevertheless, only more covertly.[5]

Open-air fish market in the Philippines.

Fortunately, as the desire for shrimp has increased, some consumers are also becoming more aware of their options and using their purchasing power to push for change. However, sources for 'clean' products are growing fewer and fewer, as there are virtually no regulations, and unscrupulous producers find new ways to skirt whatever guidelines are in place. These are not merely trivial concerns or details for the food-obsessed – where our food comes from carries ethical, environmental and possibly health implications. Environmentalists, humanitarians and public health officials around the globe warn of the dire consequences both now and into the future if the current situation continues unabated. Educated consumers can, and must, demand changes that prohibit the exploitative practices and limit the damage to the environment. It is the only way to ensure that today's supply is protected and that the beloved shrimp exists for future generations to enjoy.

Buying Basics:
Some Things to Think
About When Buying Shrimp

When selecting shrimp, the most important part is sourcing it from a reputable company that farms and fishes responsibly. The shrimp industry today is a bit like the Wild West. There are almost no enforced rules. And where there are rules, there are a lot of loopholes. Shrimp come from many different places in the world, and are raised or fished under many different conditions. They also go by many different names, as there are no standards about how to identify them. Even when consumers try to be conscientious and ask direct questions, they do not always get a straight answer. Often the restaurant or shop where they are being sold does not even know the exact provenance of the shrimp they are selling, because it is very easy to legally obfuscate the origins at every step in the process of getting the end product to the consumer. As of this writing, any shrimp that has been processed in any way is exempt from Country of Origin and farm versus wild labelling requirements. Most shrimp fall into that exempt category; processing includes deveining, peeling, freezing, beheading, packaging and cooking.

Seals of approval from watchdog groups help to ensure that the purveyor works cleanly and sustainably. Farms can leave a toxic footprint, from destruction of the mangrove forests to the chemicals and antibiotics used to keep the over-crowded, unsanitary ponds disease-free. Wild-caught shrimp can be a better choice, although they also have an environmental impact. Shrimp boats trawl in open waters, and more than half their catch is other marine life, which is known as 'by-catch', and ends up getting thrown away.

Most experts recommend buying frozen shrimp. It is frozen at sea, when it is the freshest. If you are buying shrimp that are not frozen, and you cannot be absolutely positive that they have just been pulled from the water, chances are that they have been defrosted. In any case, examine them closely. Shrimp should not be broken, slimy, falling apart or mushy. They should look shiny and translucent and be firm to the touch. They should not smell of ammonia or be 'off' in any way.

Frozen shrimp can be purchased year round. They can be individually frozen or frozen in blocks. Unless you will be using the entire packet, choose individually frozen shrimp, as it makes them easier to portion out. Check to see that they have not accumulated frost, which means they have been subjected to changes in temperature. Bags should be clean and not ripped or opened.

Shrimp are usually sold by weight. Shrimp are carefully sized and will be very uniform. This is done on purpose. Restaurants purchase shrimp according to how many are in a pound, and restaurants like to spend money wisely. Generally speaking, the smaller the number, the bigger the shrimp. In the international classification system used by packers and producers, u10 is the smallest number, which means there are fewer than ten shrimp per pound (450 g); these are the largest shrimp – some would say 'super' or 'extra colossal'. Furthermore, the larger the shrimp, the more expensive they are. The U10s are more expensive than the smaller varieties. So keep yield in mind when purchasing. Also, remember that once peeled you will lose up to half of the weight. So, 1 kg (2.2 lb) of unpeeled shrimp will equal ½ kg (1.1 lb) of peeled shrimp, or about 2 cups.

A good rule of thumb for guessing the number of shrimp per pound are the following quantities:

Small: 51 or more per pound
Medium: 36–50 per pound
Large: 26–40
Jumbo: 16–25
Colossal: 10–15

These are not standard units of measurement and will vary by producer or seller. Rather, they are just meant as a guideline. Let your recipe be your guide as to which size to buy. In a shrimp cocktail or on a tray of hors d'oeuvres large, dramatic-looking shrimp will seem impressive, but in salads or pastas, smaller, bite-size shrimp that are easier to eat, and which guarantee a piece in every forkful, are usually better.

Melanosis is a black discolouration or spots which start to appear on shrimp after they have been harvested. They are similar to the brown spots that appear on fruit when it is past its prime. They emerge first on the head and then on the body. Their appearance does not necessarily mean the shrimp have spoiled, but they are not likely to be the freshest either. Sulphites are sometimes used to prevent this from happening, but there are strict limits as to how much can be used because some people are allergic to them. Labels require that packaging indicate if sulphites have been used. In addition, other additives can be used to make shrimp retain water, thus making them seem bigger and allowing the seller to charge more for them. When given the option, buy shrimp with no additives.

Always defrost them in the refrigerator or under cold running water. They can also be defrosted by placing them in a bowl of cold water. Never defrost them in warm water. This is a toxic bacterial soup. Shrimp can be contaminated with Salmonella and Vibrio, among other things. Always discard waste and wash hands and surfaces and tools with hot, soapy water after handling raw or defrosted shrimp.

Shrimp, once defrosted, will spoil quickly. Keep them refrigerated until ready to cook, and use within 24 hours. For more information, see the websites and associations listed at the end of this book.

Recipes

Prawn Wiggle

Frank Schloesser, *The Cult of the Chafing Dish* (London, 1904)

This is an American recipe and rejoices in the name of 'Prawn Wiggle'. Melt three tablespoons of butter in the dish, and two tablespoons of flour mixed with a teaspoon of salt and a good pinch of pepper. Stir up and then pour in gradually half a pint of milk. As soon as the sauce thickens add a cupful of prawns and a cupful of cold cooked green peas. Mix up well and simmer for eight minutes. The pink and green form a delightsome colour blend, suggesting certain well-known racing colours, and the combined flavours are most delicate. But why 'wiggle'? Well, why not?

Prawns on the Grass

Frank Schloesser, *The Cult of the Chafing Dish* (London, 1904)

Prawns on the Grass is recommendable, easy and decorative for the supper table. Butter lightly the bottom of the Chafing Dish, half fill it with carefully prepared cooked cold spinach; on this put a dozen prawns, two eggs, hard-boiled and cut in quarters; arrange these symmetrically, add pepper, salt and a cupful of milk. Cover up and let it simmer steadily for ten to twelve minutes. Serve in the Chafing Dish with sippets of toast.

Shrimp Cocktail
Grand Forks Herald (1919)

1 can shrimp
1–2 cups tomato ketchup
1–2 cups sherry wine
4 tbsp lemon juice
2 tsp Tabasco sauce
1–2 tsp finely chopped chives
1 tsp salt

Soak shrimps in ice water for fifteen minutes. Drain on a dry towel. Remove the veins and cut into small pieces. Add the seasoning. Mix well and serve in cocktail glasses.
Serves 6–8

Shrimp Cocktails
The Bystander (London, 1922)

Put into the bottom of a rather large wine glass, a good dessertspoonful of tomato sauce, cover with picked shrimps, and then add a dessertspoonful of Worcestershire sauce, in which a few drops of Tabasco pepper sauce has been added. The latter is an American sauce, and gives the requisite hot flavour to the cocktail.

Shrimp Sauce
Boston Cooking School Magazine (1900)

Answer to a reader's query for a 'Recipe for shrimp sauce served with shad roe; not a drawn-butter sauce – something more delicate, with a suspicion of sherry about it'
Prepare a drawn-butter sauce with one-fourth a cup, each, of butter and flour and one pint of well-seasoned fish stock; cook on a corner of the range, where it bubbles occasionally on one side,

half an hour or more; skim off the butter carefully and add half a cup of sherry or Madeira, and a cup of picked shrimps with a teaspoonful of lemon juice; a tablespoonful of shrimp butter may be added also, if desired.

Shrimp Tropicana

Can-venient Ways with Shrimp: Delightful . . . Delicious . . . and Deveined
(U.S. Department of the Interior, Washington, DC, 1966)

2 cans shrimp (4½ or 5 oz. [125 g] each)
1 cup (225 g) creamed cottage cheese
½ cup (100 g) drained crushed pineapple
⅓ cup (75 ml) mayonnaise or salad dressing
2 tsp lemon juice
½ tsp salt
6 lettuce leaves
12 slices buttered cracked wheat bread

Drain shrimp and rinse with cold water. Chop shrimp. Drain cottage cheese. Combine all ingredients except lettuce and bread. Chill. Spread six slices of bread with approximately ⅓ cup shrimp mixture. Cover with lettuce and remaining six slices of bread.
Serves 6

Mrs Lyndon B. Johnson's
Recipe for Shrimp Squash Casserole

Lyndon Baines Johnson was the 36th President of the United States, from 1963 to 1969. His wife, known as Lady Bird, probably spent little time in the kitchen. But somebody has collected her recipes and they are housed at the LBJ Presidential Library in Austin, Texas. This is her contribution to shrimp in casserole dishes.

3 cups (450 g) yellow squash
¾ cup (140 g) raw shrimp

2 tbsp margarine
2 tbsp flour
½ tsp salt
⅛ tsp pepper
1 cup (250 ml) chicken broth
½ cup (120 ml) whipping cream
1 tbsp finely minced onion
½ cup (60 g) coarse breadcrumbs
¼ cup (25 g) grated parmesan cheese
1 tbsp melted margarine

Wash and dry squash. Cut crosswise into ¼-inch slices. Thoroughly rinse shrimp under cold water and drain. Heat two tablespoons of margarine in sauce pan. Blend in flour, salt and pepper, cook until it bubbles. Remove from heat and add chicken broth gradually stirring constantly. Bring to a boil for one or two minutes. Blend in cream and minced onions. Mix in raw shrimp. Layer squash in 1½-quart casserole dish. Spoon half of shrimp sauce over squash. Repeat with remaining squash and shrimp sauce. Cover tightly and place in a 400 degree oven for 30 minutes. Meanwhile toss bread-crumbs and Parmesan cheese with melted margarine. After 30 minutes, top squash/shrimp with breadcrumbs. Reduce oven heat to 350 degrees and return casserole to oven for 15 minutes or until crumbs are golden brown.

Tom Yam Kung Soup (Spicy Lemony Shrimp Soup)
This is a classic soup from Thailand.

680 g (1½ lb) medium-sized uncooked shrimp (U25)
2.5 l (2½ quarts) water
1 tablespoon dried lemongrass sticks cut into 3 cm (1 inch) lengths
80 ml (⅓ cup) strained fresh lime juice
80 ml (⅓ cup) *nam pla* (Thai fish sauce)
60 ml (¼ cup) finely cut fresh coriander
or cilantro leaves

60 ml (¼ cup) thinly sliced spring onion (scallion) tops cut into strips about 3 mm (⅛ inch) wide and 3 cm (1 inch) long
2–3 fresh red Thai chillies, chopped

Shell and devein the shrimp, leaving tails attached. Wash shrimp under cold running water and pat them completely dry with paper towels.

In a heavy, 4-litre (4–6 quart) casserole, bring water to a boil over high heat. Drop in the lemongrass and boil uncovered for about ten minutes or until the leaves become somewhat yellow. Stir in lime juice and *nam pla* and boil for an additional five minutes. Reduce heat to medium, drop in the shrimp and cook for four or five minutes longer until shrimp are firm and pink. Add fresh coriander leaves, spring onion tops and red chillies. Serve immediately.

Serves 6

Monti Carlo's Tropical Shrimp Ceviche

Monti Carlo is a Food Network Personality, food blogger and recipe developer. She is a proud Puerto Rican that loves all things related to the cuisine of her homeland: *la Cocina criolla*. She lives in Los Angeles.

A tropical pickled shrimp salad makes for a cool and refreshing lunch. In this recipe use 500 g (1 lb) of 26/30 shrimp; they cook up bite-sized, a wonderful choice for a summer salad.

This is a ceviche-style shrimp salad. The acidic dressing cooks them all the way through. It's always best to lightly poach shrimp for two or three minutes first, to kill bacteria that citrus can't. After poaching, pickle the shrimp in a bitter orange passion fruit dressing for thirty minutes and then remove them from the dressing so they don't become rubbery. Pour the dressing into a bowl filled with shredded green papaya, purslane and shallot and let them soak up the citrusy liquid. Add mango, coriander (cilantro) and gooseberries for a colourful, tropical punch then garnish with creamy avocado and crispy plantain chips.

Purslane (in case you're not familiar with it) is a succulent with a juicy, crisp bite and green apple flavour. It's a weed that's rich in omega-3s and grows wild throughout much of the world. You can find it along with all of the tropical fruits for this salad in your favourite Latino grocery store where it might be known as *verdolagas*. It is also known as pigweed, little hogweed, redroot, pursley and moss rose. If you have trouble sourcing purslane you can substitute with another hearty green like watercress or arugula. Treat green papaya like you would a vegetable. Look for fruit that is deep green and heavy for its size. It shouldn't have any soft spots. The texture and flavour of green papaya can be mimicked by julienning a small head of cabbage along with 1 small jicama also known as Mexican yam bean or Mexican turnip. When jicama isn't available you can sub green apples in the slaw. Tangy, orange Cape gooseberries are also known as uchuva, golden berry or Inca berry. They are related to the tomatillo and can come still covered in their beige papery husk. Remove the husk and rinse them before cutting them in half. Good substitutes include rainier cherries, orange grape tomatoes or tomatillos.

Monti says,

> I grew up in Mayaguez, a town in Puerto Rico known for its delicious mangoes. I find that the smaller, golden Champagne mangoes have the best sweetness and texture. These mangoes are also known as Ataulfo and their creamy flesh has huge notes of honey. They are much more flavourful than larger mangoes which can be fibrous and taste watered-down. Choose mangoes with a strong perfume which have some give when you press a finger into them. If you can't find mango, you can always sub in figs or peaches. The following recipe makes 6 servings of cool, refreshing, tangy tropical shrimp salad. *Buen provecho*!

For poaching shrimp:
2 l water
3 to 4 tbsp of salt
75 g (½ cup) dried shrimp (optional)
3 dried spicy red chillies
1 tsp black peppercorns

1 bay leaf
500 g (1 lb) 26/30 shrimp

For pickled salad:
1 green papaya, julienned (substitute with jicama or 2 green
apples and 1 small head of cabbage)
300 g (2 cups) purslane leaves, cleaned (substitute watercress or
arugula)
1 shallot, thinly sliced in half moons
zest of 3 limes (about 2 to 3 tsp)
8 limes, juiced
4 lemons, juiced
1 orange, juiced
120 ml (½ cup) passionfruit pulp (to keep cost down use frozen
pulp, found in the fruit section of Latino groceries' frozen foods
aisles. If using fresh pulp, strain out the seeds.)
2 tbsp extra virgin olive oil
2 habaneros, seeded, deveined and minced
2 tsp garlic, minced
¼ tsp anchovy paste
¼ tsp ginger, minced

For tropical fruit salad:
2 champagne mangos sliced into half moons ¼ inch thick
3 heaping tbsp of coriander (cilantro) leaves
150 g (1 cup) gooseberries, sliced in half
1 tbsp extra virgin olive oil
1 tsp lime juice
¼ tsp lime zest
salt and ground red pepper to taste
plantain chips for garnish
thinly sliced avocado for garnish (brush with citrus dressing to
prevent oxidization)

Place 2 litres of salted water in a large pot over high heat. Add salt
until it tastes like the sea, about 3 tablespoons. Add the optional
dried shrimp and the red chillies. While the water comes up to a

boil rinse the pound of defrosted shrimp in cool water. Remove from shells. Add the shells to the broth. Rinse shrimp and set in a bowl along with ½ teaspoon of salt and set aside.

Once the broth comes to a boil, lower the heat to medium and simmer for ten minutes so that the flavours develop. Prepare an ice bath. Add the shrimp to the simmering broth and immediately turn off the heat. Gently stirring, poach the shrimp for two minutes or until they are about 50 per cent opaque. Remove shrimp and place in ice bath for a few minutes to stop any carry-over cooking. Remove from the ice bath and dry on paper towels. Strain the shrimp shell broth and refrigerate once it's cool. Use it to poach eggs later.

Prepare the bitter orange passion fruit dressing. Bitter orange grows wild in Puerto Rico and is often used to tenderize and flavour meats. You can mimic its flavour profile by mixing ½ part orange juice with 1 part lemon and 4 parts lime. Zest and juice 8 limes. Reserve 2 teaspoons of zest and store the rest. Zest and juice 1 orange and 4 lemons. Store their zest for future use. You should have about 350 ml (1½ cups) of liquid. Add frozen passion fruit purée and stir until incorporated.

Using a mortar and pestle or small food processor purée olive oil, garlic, habaneros, anchovy paste, salt and pepper to taste. Add to the citrus juice mix and blend.

Remove shrimp from ice bath and place in a non-reactive bowl. Mix the shrimp with the dressing and cover in plastic wrap. Refrigerate for thirty minutes or until cooked through.

Rinse the papaya to clean it. Lay the papaya on its side and slice off the stem end. Stand the papaya on this end and use a potato peeler to remove the deep green skin. Slice the papaya in half, from top to bottom. Scrape out the white seeds.

Use a mandoline to julienne the papaya lengthwise into ½ cm (⅛ inch) thick strips. If you don't have a mandoline GET ONE. Check Asian markets for great deals. Otherwise use a julienne peeler or your chef's knife to shred the papaya.

Place the shredded papaya in a colander. And put that colander over a bowl. Mix 1 teaspoon of sugar into 2.5 teaspoons of salt and sprinkle over the papaya. Let papaya sit for ten minutes or so until limp. Reserve the liquid in the bowl. Rinse the papaya in the colander with cold water and then place it in the centre of a food-safe dish towel.

Remove excess liquid by wrapping the dish towel around the mound of papaya and twisting the ends together until papaya milk starts to soak through the towel. Holding the papaya above the bowl where you have reserved its liquid, squeeze as much milk out of the papaya as you can and into the bowl. Save this liquid and use it as a natural meat tenderizer. Place the now dried shredded papaya into a non-reactive bowl. Mix in the purslane and thinly sliced shallot.

Remove shrimp from dressing and adjust the dressing seasoning for salt and heat. Mix in 1 teaspoon of lime zest. Pour the dressing into the bowl that contains your shredded papaya. Let the papaya and greens soak it in for at least ten minutes.

Slice a mango lengthwise along both sides of the seed. Cut those two slices in half again, lengthwise. Separate the flesh by running a spoon between it and the skin. Slice the mango into 5 cm (2 inch) slices about 1 cm (¼ inch) thick. Wash gooseberries and cut in half. Rinse cilantro in a bowl of cold water and then dry. Mix in the cilantro with the mango and gooseberries. Dress this salad with olive oil, lime juice, salt and red pepper.

Plate a scoop of green papaya salad with three to four shrimp on top, adding 2 tablespoons of the cilantro tropical fruit salad to the plate. Garnish with avocado and plantain chips.

Terry's Shrimp Bisque

1.5 kg (3 lb) head-on shrimp
3 tbsp unsalted butter
1 small onion, diced
1 medium carrot, peeled and diced
1 medium stalk celery, diced
1 tbsp tomato paste
1 bay leaf
1 litre (4 cups) water

1.5 tbsp plain (all-purpose) flour
60 ml (¼ cup) sherry
180 ml (¾ cup) heavy whipping or double cream
dash of cayenne pepper
dash of ground nutmeg
sea salt
ground black pepper

First, make the shrimp stock by dry steaming the shrimp. Place shrimp, shells and heads on, in a dry stock pot over medium heat. Do not season. Once shrimp release their juices, remove from heat and shake the pot vigorously until they turn pink. Cool until they can be handled, remove shells and set aside. Chop the shrimp into bite sizes and keep cold.

Over medium heat, melt a third of the butter in a small stock pot. Add carrots, onion, celery and shrimp shells. Cook, stirring occasionally, until onion begins to soften and shells caramelize. Add tomato paste and bay leaf and stir, coating everything evenly. Add water and stir to combine. Heat and simmer for about thirty minutes.

Remove from heat and strain liquid into clean bowl. Set aside. This is your shrimp stock. Clean pot and return to stove. Melt the remaining butter and add flour. Whisk until flour becomes golden, about three to four minutes.

Slowly add sherry and shrimp stock, whisking to smooth. Bring to a simmer and add cream, cayenne, nutmeg and chopped shrimp. Add salt and pepper to taste. Warm until flavours meld and soup thickens, about five minutes. Serve immediately or chill until needed and reheat.

Serves 8–10

Gulf Coast Seasoning Mix

'Old Bay Seasoning' is a proprietary spice blend and very popular in the southern u.s. If not available, this makes a good substitute:

1 tbsp celery seeds

1 tbsp whole black peppercorns

6 bay leaves

½ tsp whole cardamoms

½ tsp mustard seeds

4 whole cloves

1 tsp sweet Hungarian paprika

¼ tsp mace or nutmeg

In a spice grinder or small food processor, combine all of the ingredients. Grind well and store in a small glass jar. Best if used within six months (date the jar).

Belgian Shrimp Croquettes

Popular at beaches in Belgium – once a working-class meal, now a pricey entrée.

500 g (1 lb) medium shrimp, cooked in salted water and drained (reserve 120 ml [½ cup] of the cooking water)

2 tbsp unsalted butter

½ small finely chopped onion

40 g (¼ cup) plus 3 tbsp plain (all-purpose) flour

250 ml (1 cup) milk

2 egg yolks

300 g fine dried breadcrumbs made from soft white bread

½ tsp salt

⅛ tsp cayenne

⅛ tsp nutmeg

1 egg

vegetable oil for deep frying

Peel and devein the shrimp. Chop finely. Set aside. Melt the butter in a saucepan over medium heat. Add the onions and cook for about two minutes, or until wilted. Add the 3 tablespoons of the flour and stir. Add the milk and the shrimp liquid, stirring constantly with a whisk until the mixture is thick and smooth. Continue cooking, stirring constantly for two minutes. Add the shrimp and egg yolks, stirring constantly, cook for about thirty seconds. Add half of the breadcrumbs, salt, cayenne and nutmeg. Cool thoroughly. Divide the mixture into sixteen equal portions. Shape each portion into a small ball. Roll the balls in the remaining flour. Beat the egg with some of the reserved shrimp cooking water. Roll the croquettes in the egg mixture and then in the remaining breadcrumbs. Press to help the crumbs adhere. Shake off any excess. Heat the oil to high for deep-fat frying. Fry the croquettes, three to four minutes, or until they are golden brown. Drain on paper towels. Serve immediately.

References

1 What's in a Name?
The Biology and Biography of the Shrimp

1 'Anatomy of a Shrimp: Glossary and Illustrations',
  Shrimp News International, www.shrimpnews.com,
  accessed April 2016.
2 Jack and Anne Rudloe, *Shrimp: The Endless Quest for Pink
  Gold* (Upper Saddle River, NJ, 2009), pp. 15–26.
3 Wyss Institute, 'Shrilk Biodegradable Plastic',
  http://wyss.harvard.edu, accessed May 2017.

2 How We Do Love Thee

1 Robert I. Curtis, 'In Defense of Garum', *Classical Journal*,
  LXXVIII (1983), pp. 232–40.
2 Reverend J. G. Wood, MA, 'Shrimps and Prawns',
  The Argosy: A Magazine of Tales, Travels, Essays, and Poems
  (July 1886), pp. 24–30.
3 Peter Brears, *All the King's Cooks* (London, 1999),
  p. 145.
4 Robert May, *The Accomplish't Cook* (London, 1660).
5 'Cookery', *Magazine of Domestic Economy*, IX (1839).
6 'Potted Shrimps' and 'to Pickel Shrimps', in *Johnson Family
  Cookbook* (1694–1831), Wellcome Library Cookbook Archive.

7 J.G.B., 'Minor Crustacean Dainties', *The Graphic* (26 April 1890), p. 475.

3 Fashion Plates: Shrimp Cocktail on Ice

1 *Kentish Bell's Literary Intelligence and New National Omnibus*, 8 February 1834, p. 7.
2 '65 Years of Mississippi Seafood History', *Daily Herald*, 3 July 1933, p. 16.
3 Deanne Stephens Nuwer, '"The Biloxi Fishermen are Killing the Goose that Laid the Golden Egg": The Seafood Strike of 1932', *Journal of Mississippi History*, LXVI (2004), pp. 324–52.
4 'Shrimp Illiterates', *Daily Herald*, 30 January 1922, p. 2.
5 'Fish is Certainly Fine Brain Food for the Fisherman', *The Pueblo Chieftain*, 16 March 1918, p. 9.
6 Julia Moskin, 'A Thread of Pride in a Round of Shrimp', *New York Times*, 21 November 2012.

4 Powder and Paste and a Sense of Place

1 Robert I. Curtis, 'In Defense of Garum', *Classical Journal*, LXXVIII (1983), pp. 232–40.
2 Levi van Sant, 'Lowcountry Visions: Foodways and Race in Coastal South Carolina', *Gastronomica: The Journal of Critical Food Studies*, XV (2015), pp. 18–26.
3 Rafael Steinberg, *The Cooking of Japan* (New York, 1969).

5 Jumbo Shrimp and Other Tidbits: Shrimp in Art, Literature and Society

1 David P. Pierson, 'A Show About Nothing: Seinfeld and the Modern Comedy of Manners', *Journal of Popular Culture*, XXXIV (2004), pp. 49–64.

2 'Shrimps and Shrimpers', *The Graphic* (August 1879).

3 James Greenwood, 'To the Shrine of the Shrimp', in *Odd People in Odd Places; or, The Great Residuum* (London, 1883).

4 Francis Augustus MacNutt, *Fernando Cortes, His Five Letters of Relation to the Emperoror Charles V* (Cleveland, OH, 1908), vol. 1, pp. 233–4.

5 Marjorie, 'The Woman's Sphere', *The Sphere* (London), 20 December 1924.

6 Jess Cartner-Morley, 'Shrimps Faux Fur the Coats to be Seen in', *The Guardian*, 6 March 2014.

7 Carl A. Shaw, '"Genitalia of the Sea": Seafood and Sexuality in Greek Comedy', *Mnemosyne*, LXVII (2014), pp. 554–76.

8 'New Yorks Beat Chicago', *New York Times*, 27 September 1901.

9 'Skinny Uses Explosive Language', U.S. Boys in *Washington Times*, 13 November 1919.

10 Anatoly Liberman, 'A Scrumptious Shrimp with a Riddle', www.blog.oup.com, April 2012.

11 'The Singing Shrimps: Choir Boys from the Slums', *Evening News* (London), 2 March 1936.

6 All We Can Eat:
The High Cost of Cheap Shrimp

1 Herbert R. Padgett, 'The Sea Fisheries of the Southern United States: Retrospect and Prospect', *Geographical Review*, LIII (1963), pp. 22–39.

2 Ben G. Blount, 'Marginalization of African-Americans in Marine Fisheries of Georgia', *Urban Anthropology and Studies of Cultural Systems and World Economic Development*, XXIX (2000), pp. 285–313.

3 World Wildlife Fund Farmed Shrimp, www.worldwildlife. org, accessed June 2016.

4 Kimberly Warner et al., 'Shrimp: Oceana Reveals Misrepresentation of America's Favorite Seafood', *Oceana* (October 2014).

5 Lewis W. Hine, 'Child Labor in Gulf Coast Canneries: Photo-graphic Investigation Made February, 1911', *Annals of the American Academy of Political and Social Science*, XXXVIII (1911), pp. 118–22.

Select Bibliography

Bauer, Raymond T., *Remarkable Shrimps: Adaptations and Natural History of the Carideans* (Norman, OK, 2005)

Freedman, Paul, ed., *Food: The History of Taste* (Berkeley and Los Angeles, CA, 2007)

Grimm, Veronika, 'The Good Things That Lay at Hand', in *Food: The History of Taste*, ed. Paul Freedman (Berkeley and Los Angeles, CA, 2007)

Levenstein, Harvey, *Revolution at the Table: The Transformation of the American Diet* (New York, 1988)

Livingston, A. D., *Strictly Shrimp: A Passionate Guide to the World's Favorite Seafood* (Short Hills, NJ, 2001)

Philpott, Tom, 'As if Slavery Weren't Enough, 6 Other Reasons to Avoid Shrimp', *Mother Jones Online*, January 2016, at www.motherjones.com

Rudloe, Jack and Anne Rudloe, *Shrimp: The Endless Quest for Pink Gold* (Upper Saddle River, NJ, 2010)

Steinberg, Rafael, *The Cooking of Japan* (New York, 1969)

van Sant, Levi, 'Lowcountry Visions: Foodways and Race in Coastal South Carolina', in *Gastronomica: The Journal of Critical Food Studies*, XV (2015), pp. 18–26

Wilson, Bee, *Consider the Fork: A History of How We Cook and Eat* (New York, 2012)

Yu, Su-Mei, 'A Lamentation for Shrimp Paste', *Gastronomica: The Journal of Critical Food Studies*, IX (2009), pp. 53–6

Websites and Associations

American Shrimp
www.americanshrimp.com
Advocacy group for American shrimp concerns
with links to other commercial interests

Aquaculture Stewardship Council
www.asc-aqua.org

Environmental Justice Foundation (EJF)
http://ejfoundation.org
The Environmental Justice Foundation is a UK-based
non-profit organization working internationally to protect
the environment and defend human rights

FishWise
www.fishwise.org
A sustainable seafood consultancy that promotes
the health and recovery of ocean ecosystems through
environmentally responsible practices

Food and Water Watch Safe Seafood Guide
www.foodandwaterwatch.org

Marine Stewardship Council
www.msc.org

Monterey Bay Aquarium's Seafood Watch
www.seafoodwatch.org
An interactive website/app to track seafood sustainability and
responsible practices for all seafood, including shrimp

National Fisheries Museum, Oostduinkerke, Belgium
www.navigomuseum.be/en

National Marine Fisheries Service Fisheries of the U.S.
www.st.nmfs.noaa.gov

Naturland
A guidebook, in English, on German standards for organic
aquaculture is available at www.naturland.de

Prints of Japan
www.printsofjapan.com
A commercial site that sells fine art reproductions,
but is wonderful for browsing artwork from Japan, and
reading about the use of shrimp motifs in a variety of
fine-art applications over centuries of Japanese history

Seamark
www.seamark.co.uk
One of the largest shrimp processers in the world

The Solidarity Center
www.solidaritycenter.org
Workers' rights organization

World Wildlife Fund Farmed Shrimp
www.worldwildlife.org/industries/farmed-shrimp

South Carolina Seagrant Consortium
www.scseagrant.org

Acknowledgements

I would like to recognize and express my gratitude to several people and institutions who in some way aided me in the preparation of this manuscript. Terry Thiel ably assisted me in the research and editing of the historical recipes, as well as adding her considerable culinary expertise. Monti Carlo graciously and enthusiastically took time away from her many projects and contributed an original recipe for inclusion here, and Justin Lane took excellent photos. Chuck Florio allowed me to use his gorgeous fine art photographs of shrimp boats in Beaufort, South Carolina, and shared his knowledge of shrimp fishing with me. Peggy Florio has caught, headed, peeled, deveined and cooked thousands of 'swimps', over dozens of hours, only to watch them disappear in a handful of minutes. We all thank her.

The electronic and paper collections of some world-class libraries also made this book possible. Great thanks go to the Rutgers University library system, the British Library and the Wellcome Library, as well as the taxpayers, funders and contributors that keep these crucial sources open and available. I am grateful to series editor Andy Smith and publisher Michael Leaman at Reaktion Books for this opportunity. Personal thanks to Dave Edwards for being a sport, to Fred and Kerstin McKitrick with whom I have consumed more of everything than is advisable, to Chuck and Peggy Florio for teaching me how to eat, to Devin and Ross Lane for making everything funnier, and for Doug Lane, who in ways great and small, makes everything possible.

Photo Acknowledgements

The author and publishers wish to express their thanks to the below sources of illustrative material and/or permission to reproduce it.

© Afe207/Dreamstime.com: p. 83 (top); © Alexshalamov/Dreamstime.com: p. 91; collection of the author: pp. 15, 25, 32, 33, 34, 35, 36, 37, 40, 42, 45, 60, 72, 75, 76, 78, 82 (top); © Dreambigphotos/Dreamstime.com: p. 51; © Val C. Florio: p. 20; © Frameangel/Dreamstime.com: p. 83; courtesy J. Paul Getty Museum, Malibu, CA: p. 27; © Jamesbox/Dreamstime.com: p. 85; © Jill Battaglia/Dreamstime.com: p. 61; Library of Congress, Washington, DC: pp. 46, 47, 87, 88, 89, 90; © Marc Hufnagl: p. 13; Metropolitan Museum of Art: pp. 66, 70; © National Museum of Wales: p. 71; New York Public Library: p. 69; © Noomhh/Dreamstime.com: p. 57; © Paulbrighton/Dreamstime.com: p. 60; © Pierivb/Dreamstime.com: p. 86; © Richard Gunion/Shootalot/Dreamstime.com: p. 17; © Searagen/Dreamstime.com: p. 82 (bottom); © Morgan Sturgeon: pp. 21, 54, 55, 56, 58, 73, 74; © Tomboy2290/Dreamstime.com: p. 14; © Victoria and Albert Museum, London: pp. 30, 68.

Index

italic numbers refer to illustrations; **bold** to recipes